Kitchen Chaos

WYATT WILKINSON

Kitchen Chaos
Copyright © 2021 by Wyatt Wilkinson

All rights reserved. No part of this publication may be reproduced, distributed, or transmitted in any form or by any means, including photocopying, recording, or other electronic or mechanical methods, without the prior written permission of the author, except in the case of brief quotations embodied in critical reviews and certain other non-commercial uses permitted by copyright law.

ISBN
978-1-956529-23-4 (Hardcover)
978-1-956529-22-7 (Paperback)
978-1-956529-21-0 (eBook)

Table of Contents

Chapter 1 1

Chapter 2 11

Chapter 3 17

Chapter 4 33

Chapter 5 37

Chapter 6 47

Chapter 7 53

Chapter 8 61

Chapter 9 69

Chapter 10 75

Chapter 11 81

Chapter 12 87

Chapter 13 91

Chapter 14 97

Chapter 15 103

Chapter 16 117

Chapter 17 123

Chapter 18 131

Chapter 19 135

Chapter 20 143

Chapter 21 149

Chapter 22 161

Chapter 23 169

Chapter 24 175

Chapter 25 185

Chapter 26 191

Chapter 27 197

Chapter 28 207

Chapter 29 213

Prelude

In the world of culinary, we strive to make masterpieces you will enjoy. When you eat, it is a treat, and you want it to taste good, look appetizing, and value it.

It takes years of training, dedication and sacrifice to be a chef. We love what we do. We want you to enjoy our food and creations. As I said before, dining out is a treat and allows you to try things you can't or will not make at home for various reasons. It commemorates special occasions like birthdays, anniversaries, date nights or just some quality time with family and friends.

We eat three times a day, and it should not just be about eating to survive. We want you to enjoy it. As Chefs, we love the positive feedback. Your enjoyment is the reward. That means you will more than likely come back for more visits.

Sometimes there is no pleasing some people or working with others who are utterly oblivious to life in general. We have all seen those people. They would bitch and moan about winning a $1,000,0000. I can't figure why someone would go through life to be that unhappy.

This book is a compilation of things I have seen, experienced, or told by other chefs and hospitality professionals. They are suitable for a laugh and will make you want to cry as well. There are people out there who will amaze you. They do not have to stop and think to breathe or about any other automatic, involuntary bodily function.

Yes, we have filthy mouths, and we swear. When you encounter mind-numbing stupidity, disregard for the basics and rampant idiocy. Some things make to want to smack your head off a cinder block wall because of the lack of thought and a complete "What the fuck were you thinking?!" moment.

It is because we care about what we are doing. A perfect example would be when you are in traffic—the bone head and stupid actions cause you to have Tourette's Syndrome. When you are on the road, we use language we usually would not use as much when we see these dipshits who ought to know better than to do the shit they do. You know they have been trained better; otherwise, they would not have their driver's license in the first place. If you can relate to some of the dullards in your workplace, that makes you question their sanity and intelligence altogether. I would not be surprised if you can relate to similar incidents related to the stories in the pages ahead.

Think of this as a culinary version of Cops. Names and places have been changed to protect the guilty and the innocent.

Chapter 1

Sorry if I seem like I am going to bore you with some terms. It is essential to understand the basics before getting into the humour and the foolish mistakes in the pages ahead. However, I have added a few things for comic relief on the way to get you through it. Later, I will share stories of idiots using unfinished Mother Sauces in their creations and cooking methods to get your WTF? reactions. It is enough to make you pull your hair out or use horrific language. Given the choice and some hindsight, use the language. Your hair does not come back when you pull it out. I am almost completely bald. Do not pull your hair out. It's genetics, but if you can't laugh at yourself, you shouldn't laugh at others. I am fair game too. You'll see that ahead.

WHAT IS A CHEF?

The first thing I want to do is identify what a Chef is versus a cook. There is always confusion and discussion as to what the titles are. These were put into place by Georges Augustes Escoffier, a French Chef who developed the jobs of those working in the kitchen or, as we Chefs refer to it, as the Brigade system. The terms are French, and I have included their meanings. In smaller establishments, You may have another role brigade. The system is one of the first things you learn as a Chef. If you do not know this, you are a cook—the following an abbreviated breakdown.

Chef means Chief or head of the kitchen, which creates menus and recipes, supervises and develops staff, maintains the kitchen, and delegates duties.

Sous Chef is the second in command who is in charge when the Chef is not present.

Saucier is the sauce maker and may make the fish, finish meat dishes.

Chef de Partie manages a given station and is utilized for training staff as well.

Cuisinier or cook prepares specific dishes in a station. A perfect example is a person making pizza at an Italian station in a buffet.

Commis or junior cook usually does a specific task assisting a more senior person like the Chef de Partie.

Apprentice is usually a student learning the job and performs prep work/ cleaning and minor duties.

Plongeur or dishwasher is self-explanatory. Cleans the pots and dishes but may be utilized to do minor prep work.

Rotisseur is the Roast cook and manages that team that roasts, grills, and fries in larger establishments.

Grillardin is the grill cook.

Friturier is the fry cook.

Poissonnier is the fish cook.

Entremetier prepares soups and some other dishes not containing meat, seafood.

Potager is the soup cook and reports to the Entremetier in large kitchens.

Legumier is a vegetable cook and once again reports to the Entremetier in large kitchens.

Garde Manger is the pantry supervisor or food keeper and makes salads and other cold foods in more extensive operations, including charcuterie.

Tournant is pretty much the jack of all trades and helps wherever needed in the kitchen. They are also the breaker and covers breaks through my own experience.

Pâtissier is the pastry cook who prepares desserts, bread and other baked items.

Confiseur makes candy in more prominent places.

Glacier prepares frozen dishes like ice cream and sorbet.

Decorateur would be pretty much your show plate person and cake decorator.

Boulanger is the baker who prepares bread, cakes, and breakfast-style pastries.

Boucher is the butcher who butchers the meat, poultry and sometimes fish.

Aboyeur is the Expo that distributes orders to various stations.

Communard who prepares the meal served to the staff.

Garcon de Cuisine is the kitchen boy and performs prep work and other duties.

Interesting, there are only two positions with "Chef" in the title. If you are not the Chef or the Sous Chef, guess what? You are not a Chef. You did not earn it any more than any other rank in the military. As a private, you are not in command or any officer. It is achieved through experience and demands respect. I have fired a want-to-be chef who did not follow my directions before. Now you know the hierarchy. Also, work your pay grade. The dishwasher is not in charge. Scrub the pots and shut up.

Now here are the basic terms people should know but do not.

Doneness is the level of how thoroughly a piece of meat is cooked and its internal cooking temperature. Doneness is for meat, not pastry. Yes, I have had these orders.

Blue Rare- Very Red 115-125 F

Rare – Red Centre and soft 125-130 F I will not eat beef beyond this level.

Medium Rare- warm red starting to firm up 130-140 F.

Medium- Pink and firm 145 F. This is also the proper temperature for fish. Anything above this for seafood makes it rubbery and dry. **Never ask for well-done fish. Lamb should never go past this either**. Low-fat content will be dry and chewy—an abomination to a more expensive cut of meat.

Medium Well- a trace of pink 150-155 F

Well -Done Gray-brown, and firm 160 F (This is how your hamburger should be cooked- well-done). The only doneness for poultry pieces. You do not need to tell the Chef you want your chicken well done. There is no other option. No one wants to hear your condescending

Know-it-all and Know-nothing bullshit. Shut up. You are misinformed, and adding this arrogance to it makes you a fucking idiot.

Well done does not apply to an item like a crepe. Yes, I have had this order. It shows how stupid you are. If you want "well-done" pastry- turn your toaster to the highest setting, and there you go- charcoal.

I got told to "Keep cooking. Make it tender." Heat is dry. Meat is moist. The more you cook it, the more it dries out and the less tender it is—especially steak.

Overcooked - Blackened throughout over 160 F, usually done as a sacrifice to a deity and not intended for consumption. Pele is the Hawaiian Goddess of Fire and volcanoes. We are not sacrificing for her at Mount Kilauea at a scorching 2000 F. Everything is burnt to shit. Let my dad cook and save the travel expenses.

My dad would cook his like this. Shoe leather is tastier. Steak should not crunch! You should not have to dip it in a bath of steak sauce to choke it down. A beverage should not follow it to prevent choking and try and add any moisture to the charcoal. Charcoal is more flavorful and higher in fibre. This shit is dryer than the Sahara Desert. No one should suffer like this.

Say the Eulogy, admit it is a funeral, admit defeat and order a fucking pizza or chicken, for fuck sake. There are cruelty laws against this. Watch the food channel and learn something. Learn how to follow a fucking recipe and try again. Cooking on high is only for the appropriate methods listed below. Please follow them. You will get it and prevent further suffering.

On another note, I have been in places that insist on using thermometers to check for doneness when cooking. However, you can get a false read. Frozen chicken products like tenders, chicken burgers can do that. My best suggestion is to slice into it on an angle at the thickest point to make sure there is no pink in the chicken.

Raw chicken is a huge taboo and is unforgivable in food and beverage. Those frozen products will float in the oil when done, but I have had a few pink spots inside over the years. Check it before it goes out.

Children get chicken fingers and may not likely not be aware of the pink chicken being a bad thing. Think of those children as your own or your nieces and nephews. Do you want them getting sick from undercooked chicken? I didn't think so.

Pasta is another one of my favourite things, and I get grief on this one. All pasta is made with water, flour, semolina flour and eggs. It is then formed into sheets and cut into shapes. The exception to this rule is gluten-free pasta, usually made of rice flour or cornflour. You cannot tell me you are allergic to penne but can have spaghetti. You are not allergic to a shape.

Gluten- There is so much misinformation about this**.** I will simplify. It is a natural protein found in wheat, barley, and rye. A Celiac or persons with celiac disease have an immune reaction that causes inflammation in their intestines and can cause damage. It is painful. Approximately 1% has this condition. **Gluten-Free is not for you to lose weight**. It is a crackpot feeding you lies like all the other fad diets. It is to sell books and over-priced foods to the naïve and the gullible. Food companies never have a problem jumping on the bandwagon even though it is a fad and will fade. The name of the game is making as much as you can off the gullible and naïve quick-fix diet crowd. Eat what you want and do nothing in the form of an exercise diet crowd. I will cover this in the coming chapters.

COOKING METHODS

Roasting- a high, dry heat form f baking for meats and vegetables

Grilling- over direct heat and flames from the coals below or in industrial kitchens a charbroiler.

Braising- also my preferred method for meats like roasts. They are seared and cooked low and slow in a liquid in your roasting pan. Add a mixture of ½ onions, ¼ carrots, ¼ celery, also known as mirepoix, to the pan's bottom and cover with liquid. The water is fine. Place the meat fat side up and season with a standard salt, pepper, garlic, and a few others and for the love of God, make sure they go with the protein. Read the bottle before using—Cook Low and slow in the oven as it ensures tenderness. Pot roasts, stews fall under this method as well. If you like well-done steak, this is especially for you.
Simply put a few grill marks on it, and then in the oven with liquid it goes. It prevents choking on charcoal, as previously discussed.

Steaming- boiling water and the vapour cooks the food. This misconception is this is a wet form of cooking. False. Steam is dry. It is the water that is wet as per the confusion.

Poaching – Cooking food in liquid-like water with tiny bubbles below the boiling point.

Frying- using oil over high heat in a pan or wok and makes food taste great.

Deep Frying- Submerging food in a hot liquid. It is considered a dry method of cooking. Another misconception where the confusion sets in as the oil is liquid. If it were a wet method of cooking, your fries and onion rings would be soggy. It happens by not letting the fryer heat up correctly, and the food absorbs the oil. When this happens, it is a clear indication the cook has no fucking clue what they are doing, and you probably should go somewhere else. I insist.

Sautéing- quickly cooks thinly sliced pieces of food. I usually do this for vegetables. Low to medium heat to make the onions translucent and soft and the rest of the mirepoix (carrots and celery) and ready for the soup or stew. Low heat and cook until tender.

Stew – a form of braising for the top of the stove. Proteins are seared then added to the pot with chopped vegetables with liquid. A pot roast on the stove is stewed—lower heat for a more extended period.

Boiling- Hard boiling water or liquid with large bubbles for small-sized and delicate items like vegetables and eggs.

Baking- Cooking foods uncovered in an oven like bread, fish, chicken breasts.

Simmering- A form of stewing under boiling and usually in a covered dish.

Blanching- Partially cooked and then shocked in an ice bath to stop cooking like vegetables for the freezer. A lot of food processing places to this for frozen foods. Potatoes for your potato salad fall under this method. They are cooked to fork-tender, not mushy. Nobody wants a mushy potato salad.

Searing- small amount of fat with high heat. Best for giving colour to meat before it is stewed or braised. Caramelization.

Pasta Tip- *El Dente* This translates to the tooth. It means soft enough to chew without a crunch but firm enough where it maintains its shape. It is how it should be served. Drain and serve with your favourite sauce and cheese.

For pasta salads, shock it like the blanching process. Beyond that is mush. It falls under the same category as potato salad. Soft. Not Mushy.

Mother Sauces
There are 5 Mother Sauces, and every sauce we enjoy is a derivative of these.

Bechamel- cream sauce. Essential components are cream and roux (Equal parts flour and melted butter in a pan to form a ball and added as a thickener). Mac N Cheese starts here. Not the shit in the box.

Velouté – White roux with white stock from fish, chicken or veal used for gravies and sauces.

Espagnole – Dark roux (cooked a little longer to change colour) Brown sauce. Beef stock, tomato, deglazed beef bones. This sauce makes great gravies and other sauces like Demi glaze and is rich in flavour.

Tomato- Tomato reduction seasoned with onions and garlic. Your first one and probably everyone's favourite. Pizza comes to mind.

Hollandaise- Clarified butter and egg yolks, and it can be a pain in the ass to make. It breaks if heated for an extended period but is very tasty.

Every sauce we consume comes from one of those Mother Sauces. I have had cooks who have come through my kitchen and claimed to have gone to high-end cooking schools. There have been some who could not tell me the basic Mother Sauces. Do not try to bullshit me to impress me. If you are a liar, we will weed you out quickly.

If you cannot name the sauces, you have not been to any culinary school whatsoever. You are a fake, a fraud, a liar, and a waste of space, especially a waste of my time. It shows little respect for me to think that I would be stupid enough to believe your fucking lies and not see right through them. It is so insulting, I will fire you in minutes when I find you out, and I will do it quickly. You will last a week if you are lucky. However, I can get rid of you by the end of the day if someone else hired you. You won't make it through the interview with me without your resume going in the "Hell No" pile.

Regardless of what you have learned from your peers in high school, bullshit does not baffle brains. You will be tuned out and dismissed. You are a waste of time and effort and quickly discarded, much like the substandard food you will prepare. You are wasting food costs, which will make this type of person a liability rather than an asset.

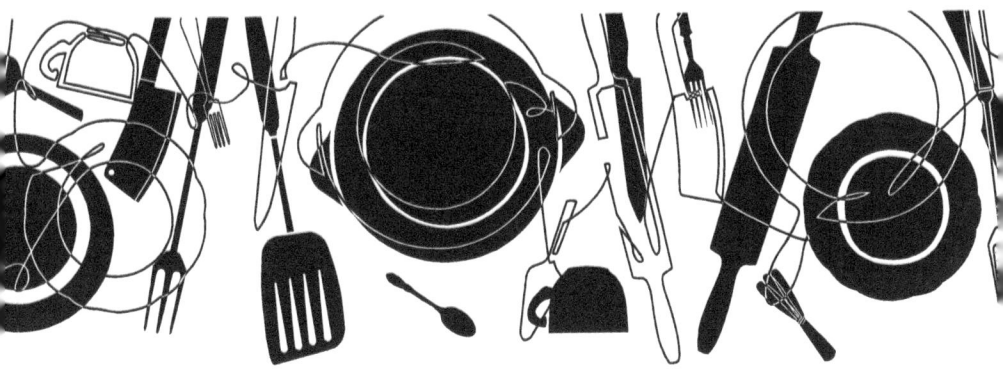

Chapter 2

I have always liked good food; however, it was not that common growing up. I grew up in a simple blue colour family where pizza was a delicacy. I started as a dishwasher and worked my way up. Family food, greasy spoon-style food all the way to resort food.

I love trying new things and fear no food. I have paid dearly in some cases and have had some vile creations that should not even be served as pet food. Straight to the bin. I have seen "creations" that will give you a "What the fuck?!" moment as they are complete culinary atrocities.

The beginning is boring. We have all seen run-of-the-mill family owner diner food of burgers, fries, hotdogs, fried chicken, meatloaf, etc. Most of that is food service and straight from the freezer. I can skip that stuff. Serving Campbell's frozen soup and adding water is not cooking. It is a food service item like frozen burgers, fries, chicken tenders, fish and chips. It works in a pinch. It is for when you are hungry and don't give a shit what you eat.

I worked in the heat and serve and even a pizza place. I have a few good ones from there. I cooked, delivered, and did a lot of the prep work. In family restaurants, the cleaning is relaxed, and you can be the scapegoat. Portion control is another issue. Eyeballing is not portioning, but many of them do it and wonder why they are not making as much money as they should.

Simply put, you are giving it away. When family members come to the restaurant and do their grocery shopping, the owners can't figure out why their food cost is out of whack. Yup, it's a mystery to me too. Stop giving it away!!

The other issue is the pricing formula is out of whack. I will cover that later. Do you think it is easy to run an operation? Think again. The industry has failures for reasons we will cover. In a nutshell- no experience, no knowledge of the industry. They think they can cook at home; they can cook for others. Nope. The food you serve at home is not food people will be willing to pay for it. Your lack of seasoning, inconsistency, improper food handling, lack of timing and cooking a single meal does not make you qualified. Sorry.

Add a full menu and numerous guests, all wanting different things at different times with special instructions. The shit disturbers are demanding free food. The waitstaff cannot time the service but must take five tables and mess the kitchen by jamming them simultaneously. The same servers that don't know the menu are sending fucked up orders with modifications that don't even make sense. Why? They are not appropriately trained.

Have you ever had dishwashers who can't get a rotation on the dishwasher to make sure the supply of clean dishes doesn't dwindle, and so on? It is all about proper training. They are failing and are "idiots" because you did not train them right. The blind leading the blind, and guess what, it is on you. Not them. Inexperienced owners always blame the staff. No wonder it's the Hindenburg. There is a lot more to it than you think. It's the tip of the iceberg, and inexperience will make you the Titanic. It will sink you.

The food and beverage industry is full of people who think they can do it better and customers who think they know more than you. Remember the well-done crepe? They ask for things that do not make sense. You will do it for them, and when it is a failure, it is on you even though they asked for it. You are serving a tangible product, and you will get complaints. It does not happen a lot, but it does happen. Ever see someone berate a fast-food worker over fries not being hot enough? Yeah? Shameful, isn't it? Shame on you if you have done it yourself.

What made you do it? If I do it, it is because they are rude or don't fucking care. Give the benefit to correct the issue. If I am going to tell them off, it is not personal. You have to use diplomacy and tact when you do it.

A lot of times, it is because of a superiority complex. It is a form of bullying. Yeah, they set out to ruin your day. Oh no, your day got ruined because you got fries that were not as hot as you want. Fries are thin and lose heat very quickly, even under the heat lamp.

You will get someone who thinks because they spent $ 10 on a fast-food meal, it is okay to be a fucking asshole to someone who works for minimum wage because they feel they are better than that loser. You are a disgrace. Oh, and you demand better service. King Shit? That loser is probably putting themselves through college or university and will be better off than you when they complete their programs.

You will be whistled at. I keep going and ignore you. I am not your fucking mutt. Snap your fingers at me. You will get the same thing. I am not coming. Yell out "Hello" in that snotty, condescending tone, and you will get the same from me, or I will continue to ignore you. I will skip right over you and go to the next person. Ever get that? Here is why. You will get the same respect you give out. Would you respond to that? No? Do not do it to someone else. Are you not coming back? Good riddance. Bye Felecia. Take it however you want it, and fuck off.

Some employers love bullying staff and have their poisonous people to back them up. Employer bullying will be covered in detail in the following pages as I was displeased with working for some on more than one occasion. They want another member of the mean club that will do their bidding in some cases. Discipline is for what they feel like doing, even if they have to make it up. Others like to keep their poisonous staff around because of time served or because they do management bidding through witch hunts. Let the trouble maker do the dirty work and reward them.

I got baptized to find my kitchen voice, according to the culinary team I was working with. This crew rode my ass, yelled and swore at me to the point where I broke. I was the dishwasher and kitchen assistant.

"Hey! Get me more vegetables," screamed one cook across the room.

"What do you need?" I shouted back. He was closest to the refrigerator. I didn't mind helping out, but it was as if they were taking advantage. I was 21 at the time.

"Carrots, celery and onions. I need it bad," he shouted.

"You are closest to the fridge. Get them yourself," I shouted back.

"No. I need you to do it," he shouted back.

"You can wait a minute. I have to get this cart out of here," I shouted back. The dirty pot cart was overflowing. These bastards did not stack anything. It was thrown on mismatch, and a lot of space was wasted. The cart could have held more. I was organizing it for transport to the dish room. I stacked the cutting boards and hotel pans accordingly. Most of the items would have been on the floor before I got six feet away in this state. Organize your carts.

I pulled the cart away and took it to the dish room. By the time I got back, the rest of the cooks were demanding more items. I had a clean cart full of hotel pans, saute pans, cutting boards, clean towels and utensils for them.

"I need hotel pans!"

"I need cutting boards!"

"I need vegetables!"

"They are here! Help yourself! I will get you fucking vegetables!" I shouted back.

"Let's go!" he shouted.

"In the time you were bitching and waiting, you could have got them yourself!" I shouted back.

"You're the kitchen attendant. It's your job!" he shouted at me.

"I got it! Keep your shirt on!" I shouted back and loaded up the small supply cart with vegetables. "Here you go!" I yelled at him. I was about three feet away, but I didn't care. This guy was a douche.

"Thank you!" Douchebag yelled in my face.

"You are welcome!" I yelled in his. This behaviour went on for a week at this new job. We were yelling back and forth within a few feet of each other. For comic relief, there was an incident when I was not wearing underwear in my white pants and shirt. I got soaked to the bone from a Cambro of water. Yes, see-through. Fuck! They thought it was hilarious. So did I. Grab a kitchen towel and cover up your front, take your little bit of dignity and exit to change your clothes. The Chef was howling. He gave me black pants and shook his head, laughing.

I came back, and the abuse continued. I was carrying a five-gallon stockpot, slipped on some spilled oil and fell. I got the recoil from stockpot in the head from my arm on the way down. I was knocked unconscious. I came back in a couple of minutes. The floor grate was embedded in my arm and bleeding. I had a nice goose egg forming on the right side of my cheek under my eye socket where I took the stockpot.

I was dizzy and covered in beans from the pot hitting me in the head. My crew came over to make sure I was still breathing. At least they showed a little compassion. The nurse came over and checked me over. I felt ok. I was a little sore for apparent reasons. I was assigned to lighter duties but asked to stay in my area in the Garde Manger (cold kitchen). I liked those assholes for some reason despite the yelling.

Garde Manger is for cold foods, salads, fruit, pates, sandwiches, cheese, and spreads like hummus. If it is prepared cold, it comes from here. They let me try some of the items. I preferred the pastry team as they were friendly and let me sample the goods too. I loved the Chef there, and he moved me up in the kitchen years later. The guy was terrific and still is. I still am eternally grateful to him. Chef Pascal. Awesome guy. I wish him the best where he may go.

The shit continued. The crew played pranks, and finally, I had enough. One kept yelling in my face.

"Just because you got knocked out, don't think I am taking it easy on you. Move your ass! Get these dishes out of here! Clean the floor! Let's go!" he was inches from my face and screaming at me.

"Fuck you!!" I was starting to cry and shake; I was so pissed off. I grabbed him by the throat. "You fucking stupid twat! I have done nothing but assist you, and all you can do is scream in my face!! You are a fucking asshole!! I have had enough of your fucking shit!!" A few of the others came over to pull me off of him. He was a lot bigger than me. I didn't care. I was taking him down. I was shaking, red in the face, crying and screaming at this asshat.

"You found your kitchen voice. Good for you. I was wondering how long it would take. You are tougher than I thought. I honestly thought you were going to quit on us. It was either that or exploded or imploded. You did both. I am surprised. It would be best if you went to sit down or you are going to have a stroke. You are very red in the face and shaking. It's not good for your health." He was talking to me like a person and not yelling.

"You did this to see what I could take?! Are you kidding me?!" I shouted.

"Yeah, to get your kitchen voice. Seriously man, get a drink and sit down. You are going to stroke out," he had sincerity in his voice. "Would someone please get him something to eat and drink and a chair?" The rest of the crew went and got me a sandwich, salad and some fruit as well as a chair. What the hell just happened?

I am still amazed when I think about that experience. I will never subject someone to that behaviour. To me, it was way over the line. I cannot think of a time where I was more hostile, hurt and pissed off. It was over the top abusive and had no place. There is a limit, and this was over it—way over the limit.

Today, when I break staff in, I use humour and get them to relax with jokes, staying within limits. I can't bring myself to go to those extremes. That cook was right; I did want to quit. I did want to smash that cook in the head with a pan. I wanted to beat him with a broom. I wanted to hurt him and badly. I wanted to see him bleed. I had him by the throat. That is not good. My advice is don't do it. You don't know the person's past, limits or mental health. Never push someone to that level.

I did report the incident but also played it down a bit. That behaviour was no longer acceptable. It was joking, but I was not in on it. It went too far. I did ask that no disciplinary action was to be taken against the crew. However, the behaviour had to be addressed and prevented.

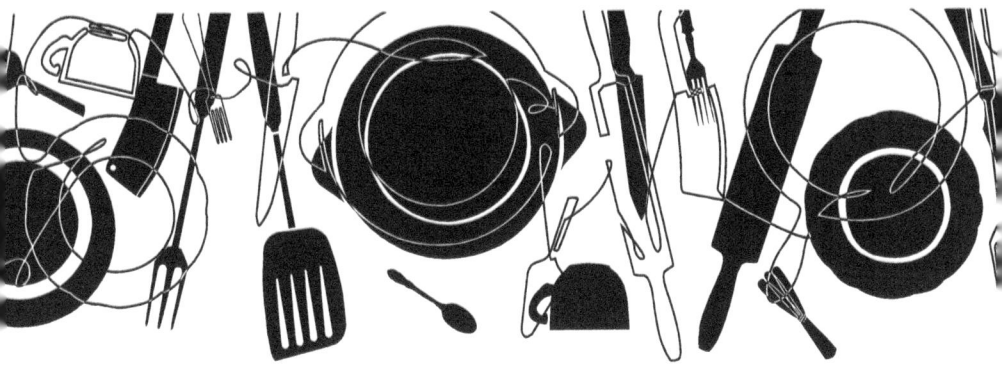

Chapter 3

I worked full-time midnights and put myself through culinary school. I talked to the head chef at the college, and he worked my schedule where I would be done by 2 PM daily. I got done work at 7 AM with my first class starting at 8 AM. It was and still is greatly appreciated. He could have said, "tough shit." It is about respect for me. I highly respect this man to this day. Thank you, Chef Mike. Yes, this is his real name. Respect. I will be using this a lot throughout the book.

I have chefs I love and respect and have complete gratitude for them as they have all contributed to where I am today. I will only use their first names. They know who they are. It is like any mentor you have had. You will carry that love and respect forever. I grew up without a dad and learned to shave from one of my friends. I will never forget it. Thanks, Al. He was respectful and took that time to help. We are here to help one another, and your actions will never be forgotten. Keep it positive.

* * *

The first Chef I worked for as a dishwasher was crass and had dark humour. I liked it. I found it hilarious. I was working near him one day at a function and accidentally bumped into him.

"Oh, sorry, Chef." I apologized.

"Don't be sorry, be more careful, or otherwise, I will be serving Braised Dishwasher tonight." He replied. He was smirking. It was an evil smirk.

"Yikes," I replied.

"No, it's okay. How much do you weigh? I need to ensure butchery and the proper cooking time," he responded with a straight face. He was looking me up and down.

"150 pounds," I replied.

"Okay, there is not as much time, so I will have to do like a 9-cut. We have over 1,000 guests tonight. You'll do just fine. I'll make you the star presentation tonight," he was smiling at me and trying not to laugh.

"Maybe another time," I replied. I require a special presentation, and you don't have the proper seasonings, plus I can marinade myself in alcohol. All I ask for is the key to the liquor cabinet," I responded. I was trying hard not to laugh too.

"Ah, good response. You'll do fine. Carry on," replied Chef and snickered. I laughed too.

* * *

In culinary school, you learn the basic knife skills of how to hold a knife properly. If you don't, your hand is going to be sore. Find the balance point between the blade and the handle just after the bolster (a piece of metal where the blade and handle meet). Your index finger and thumb will be on the top side of the blade, while the rest of your hand will be on the handle, starting with your middle finger on the bolster. It is not a hard pinch. It enables the knife to be an extension of your hand for optimum control of the blade.

When selecting your knife, you want it to be comfortable in your hand. You don't want it to be heavy, too long, and uncomfortable, as if it is like this in the trial. Imagine working with it for 8 hours. Hell.

Before you start cutting, learn how to tuck your thumb and curl your fingers to avoid cuts as much as possible. You are going to cut yourself in the kitchen. It is inevitable no matter how good you are. You will make a mistake, and you will get cut. Chef knives are very sharp and must be respected. Before attempting the cuts, please watch a video on hand curling to avoid them as much as possible and the pinch grip. If not, curl the tips of your fingers back away from the blade. That is where you will get cut, in your fingertips. We are human, and we get careless and make mistakes. Show me a chef that *never* cut himself, and I will call them a liar.

Also, it is essential to anchor your cutting board and always use one. Wet a towel, wring out the excess water and lay the towel flat on a clean counter surface. Place the cutting board on the towel. It will prevent slipping and help prevent you from cutting yourself.

In the culinary industry, our boards are colour-coded. Green is for vegetables and fruits, blue is for raw fish and seafood, red is for raw red meat, yellow is for raw chicken and poultry, white is for baked bread, cheese, and dairy, whereas tan is for cooked meats.

Always remember to wash your knives and cutting boards and your hands between items and usage. At home, you will more than likely not have coloured boards. If you cut chicken on your board, do not cut vegetables until it is washed and sanitized. Do the same for your hands. It is cross-contamination and can cause food-borne illness.

I am going to include basic cuts. Always feel free to learn more on your own through a search engine, and you will find instructional videos to help you. I am not getting paid to teach culinary school, so that it will be brief. Basic cuts include:

Large cuts= ¾ inch sticks, which can be cut into large dice ¾ inch cubes.

Medium- ½ sticks which turn to medium dice ½ inch cubes.

Batonette ¼ inch sticks to cut into small dice ¼ inch cubes.

Julienne 1/8-inch sticks to be Brunoised 1/8-inch cubes.

Fine Julienne 1/16-inch sticks to fine Brunoised 1/16-inch cubes.

Without trying to teach the entire curriculum and boring you, we use many neat tricks to get the job done. Look up dicing an onion and see how much faster it can be. One I love to show is cutting a pineapple or a melon. Fast and easy. It is well worth learning for entertaining at home.

Now back to culinary school. We partnered with other students. I was a mature student as I was over 30 and retaining for another job. My lab partner was 19. I forget his name so we will call him Jim.

Jim was doing his basic cuts, and within 20 minutes, he cut the tip of his finger and good too. Blood was pouring out of his left index finger. He just kept doing his cutting exercise while blood pooled on the board and his vegetables.

"Jesus, Jim, you cut yourself! Why are you still cutting vegetables?!" I asked in disbelief.

"I have to finish this…." He whined.

"Are you kidding me, right now?! You are bleeding all over the board and food! Do you think anyone wants your bloody vegetables?!" I could not believe this guy. I know you put blood, sweat and tears into your work, but not to be taken literally.

"Stop telling me what to do!"

"Holy fuck, man!"

"What's going on over here…." Asked the Instructor Chef. Chef Dave. He stopped mid-sentence looking at the bloody mess on the cutting board. He shook his head in disbelief. "Go see the nurse," he said, trying to hide his disgust and disbelief.

I got the fun task of cleaning up his bloody mess, disinfecting the board and his knife. Wow, just wow. It is because of this mentality and behaviour I went prematurely gray. Ever watch the cooking shows and competitions on TV? You will understand why they swear. Fuck.

The same day, another student put her big 10-inch Chef's knife in a sink full of soapy water with the cutting boards. She left to do other tasks leaving her knife in the sink. Another student went to wash the dishes. It was not long before the sink of hot water was red as he sliced his hand open from her knife. Chef Dave was pissed. He rushed over and put paper towels on his wound and got him to apply pressure, and sent him to the nurse.

"Everyone Stop!!" yelled Chef Dave. You could hear a pin drop. "Get over here and listen!" The whole class move over to where he was standing. Chef Dave had a vein bulging in his temple. Oh yes, he is pissed right off.

"You need to be more careful. That is two students on the first day for medical attention due to cuts. One working on his cuts and kept cutting! If you cut yourself, stop what you are doing and take care of the cut! The next student got cut because someone put a sharp knife in soapy water!! Whose knife is this?!" he shouted, holding the knife up.

"Mine, Chef," replied a larger red-haired girl.

"Never leave a sharp knife in soapy water. Wash your knives. If I see this again, you are out of my class. Thanks to your lack of judgment, one of your classmates cut his hand open! Knives are sharp! They DO NOT go in a sink! They go on the counter where you can see them, and they are to be washed individually by hand! They are to be washed by you and you only. Is that clear?" he scolded and held her knife by the blade extending the handle towards her.

"Yes, I am sorry..." she stammered. Nervous and embarrassed by her mistake.

"Don't be sorry. Learn from it." He said, pushing the knife towards her with his arm extended and slightly.

"Thank you, Chef," she sheepishly replied, accepting her knife. She took it and walked away like a dog with its tail between its legs. That never happened again in our class.

* * *

Culinary school is where you make your mistakes. I am going to rattle off some of mine before you think I am a pompous ass. The baking class was great. Chef Leo told me repeatedly baking is a science. Baking recipes must be followed precisely for perfect results. I have no patience. That is one of my downfalls. When you operate a mixer, patience is required. If it looked mixed to me, I got in pans and baked it. I did not always have the best results.

Now is your chance to laugh at my funniest mistake. Key lime pie. The recipe called for green food colouring. The bottle I had was not cooperating. I squeezed it hard, and then a stream of the green went into my pie filling. Patience. Yeah, far beyond the 2-3 drops required by the recipe. I had enough colouring in that bowl for the whole class and the next one too.

"Fuck!" I shouted. Naturally, all eyes are now on me and my glowing green pie filling. Chef Leo came over and started laughing. I started laughing, and so did the others around me.

"I had a bet with my wife last night this was going to happen. I did not think it was going to be you. You have to finish it now." Stated Chef Leo was holding back his laughter.

I poured it into the pie shell and let it set in the walk-in cooler. Everyone knew which one was mine. It was the one that was just short of glowing—bright fluorescent neon green Key Lime pie. Yes, patience is needed in baking.

My lowest marks were in baking. I got a B in all of them. Patience. I like to get things done. I want to take my time on decorating but am still not the best at it. I had students in the class who could pipe out some beautiful works of art in their icing. I did the standard roping, rosettes, and some carved fruit. I was not good at the roses, but my leaves turned out acceptable. Everyone has a talent for other things. I went in thinking baking would be great, but I enjoyed the cooking end more.

There were all kinds of skill levels in the classroom. We had one with a learning disability. Mario was a friendly young man, and he tried. His name was Mario. For some reason, the others did not like him. Maybe it was his directness. I thought he was okay. I still talk to him 15 years later. I made friends with him. He needed one.

I was given Mario as a lab partner. No one wanted to work with him. I was okay with it. He seemed hyper with ADHD, perhaps. Chef pulled me aside prior. He told me I might be the best lab partner for him. He told me to keep him on task. I assured him I would.

Culinary recipes are written in mind with multiple persons to feed. The recipes in our text provided around 20 persons or more. As part of the learning process, we had to adjust them to a serving of one. Math skills are required. There is a lot of math in culinary, from costing to portioning and pricing. It is not the front-of-house manager or the general manager who does the menu. Your Chef does, and he better be good with numbers and controls, or you are in serious trouble.

The assignment was cheese souffle. Souffles can be difficult if you don't follow instructions. They are not that bad. Our filling turned out great. I liked having Mario with me. He was eager to please. When he went for his ramakin, he brought me one too. He did this for everything. By the end of the day, we were a solid team. We split the tasks and went for it. How could anyone not want to work with him? They were missing out. He aimed to please and be helpful. I admire that. The drive is there and the desire to learn. He was a team player for sure.

It was going great, except we made a tiny calculation error in the bake time. We forgot to adjust it for the size of our crème Brulee-sized souffles. Yup, you guessed it. Another sacrifice to Pele. Burnt throughout and blackened beyond recognition. It was a couple of smouldering bowls of charcoal. Mario started to cry.

"Fuck!" I said quite loudly. Mario was crying even more. I was getting pissed right off. Then I heard some comments and saw some of the other students mocking him, and I even heard one of them say the word "retard". I was livid.

"Stop crying! There is no crying in the kitchen. Yeah, we fucked up. We fix it." Fuck this shit." I picked up a souffle with the oven mitt and threw it in the sink. Mario started laughing and still had some tears rolling down his face. Now it was time to get it together.

"Get us some more ramekins. I got the rest." I stated.

I went straight to the bitches next to us that called him a "retard" I snatched their bowl and took the leftover ingredients.

"Hey! You can't have that," whined the shorter, heavier girl.

"Did you hear me ask for it?" I sneered. "Since you want to be disrespectful and call him a retard, I am going to be just as rude and take what I want." I scraped out the remnants and threw the bowl back on the counter. I marched on to the next station. My body language was hostile. You do not pick on someone who can't fight back, and you sure as hell do not demean someone with a disability and call them a fucking retard. I just took what I wanted and filled the bowl enough for two souffles. They knew I was furious. Nobody got in my way. I went to every station. I glared at everyone who laughed at Mario.

Here is the reason. I have two family members with learning disabilities. I had to help my older brother with his homework in high school, and I was still in elementary school. One of his teachers dared to call him stupid. People learn in different ways. Who the Hell are you to say something like that? Seriously?! Mario was crying, and now it's fodder for entertainment?! Hell no!!

We put the souffles up together. We marched right up to the Chef's table to present. Mario was smiling. He was enormously proud of what we did. He was glowing. They looked great.

"You first," I said to Mario smiling at him.

He placed his souffle down in front of Chef. The Chef cut it open, and it was perfect. He tasted it.

"Well done, Mario. Great souffle." Mario looked over at me and smiled. I smiled back and placed mine on the table for him to try as well.

"Mario, go ahead and clean up," said Chef smiling at him. Mario walked back over to our station. He was walking tall. He was proud of himself and what we accomplished.

"I need to tell you that I saw what happened. I am proud of you. That needed to happen. They were out of line. However, your language needs to tone down a bit. I will look past that. I have never seen him so proud. He is delighted. I am giving you both a 10/10. Thank you," said Chef smiling at me. Whew! I thought I was in serious trouble. I pretty much bullied and intimidated the entire class. They had it coming.

I walked back over to Mario and helped him tidy up the station. He was packing up his books, knives, and other tools when I nudged him. He stopped. I leaned over and whispered in his ear. "We got perfect. Great job. I will be your partner any time." I pulled away. He was smiling from ear to ear. He was my lab partner for the remainder of the module. Nobody dared to disrespect him when I was around.

Before this incident, the entire class had a meeting about respect without Mario being present. Chef brought up the topic of learning disabilities and how he should not be the subject of ridicule. I never disrespected him. I tried to give him some direction, but he was not quite getting it. It was his third time taking the class. I will tell you he did graduate with me. He called it this time. Some people take a bit longer to learn or learn differently.

Just because they do not get it right away, that does not make them stupid. It means you must adjust the delivery method. Find something the person can relate to, and once you have that, they can do anything. That goes with everyone. Sometimes, it needs to be explained differently or slow down the instructions to be absorbed if you do not understand something. Just do not be a condescending asshole when you do it. No one likes to be disrespected like that and if you demand their respect for doing it, go fuck yourself. That is all of the respect you deserve for that. Respect is a two-way street, pal.

* * *

It amazes me how hard it is to follow instructions. The level of arrogance for the simplest of tasks is exhausting. We had an entire class making fresh-cut French Fries. I know some of you are thinking of just cutting the potatoes and fry them in the deep fryer. Nope.

Fresh-cut French fries require cutting potatoes but not just any potato. It would be best if you had starchy potatoes versus a waxy potato. How do I tell the difference? There are two types of potatoes: Starchy and waxy.

Starchy Potatoes are mealy such as Russets, Idahos and yams. They are high in starch and low in moisture and absorbant. They are also larger, which makes excellent fries again. These potatoes are best for baking, frying, boiling and mashing.

Waxy Potatoes are low in starch but high in sugar and moisture. They hold their shape better after cooking. They have thin skin and are smaller in size. Fingerling, Red Bliss. These potatoes are great for boiling and roasting.

All-purpose potatoes like Yukon Gold are right in the middle of the previous two types and can be used for anything. They make terrific mashed potatoes and salads. I have not tried them for French Fries, but all-purpose would indicate you can. I prefer bakers.

How to make the perfect French Fries:

1. Select your potatoes, such as an Idaho Baker.
2. Wash the skins as I find it adds to the dish. Remove the excess dirt. You do not want gritty fries.
3. Cut the potatoes into roughly half-inch squared strips, or use the French Fry cutter if you have one.
4. Soak the fries in cold water for about an hour. Soaking removes the excess starch and prevents browning.
5. Preheat deep fryer to 325 F
6. Remove fried from water and pat them dry. You do not want water in the deep fryer as it will spatter hot oil, and you can get burned, plus it makes a mess.
7. Place fries in hot oil and let them cook for 4 minutes—the blanching process.
8. Remove from fryer and place on paper towels.
9. Turn up the fryer to 375 F
10. Place the fries back in when at temperature. Cook for another 4 minutes to crisp them up.
11. Remove the fries from the fryer and place them in a mixing bowl.
12. Season with sea salt of your favourite fry seasoning and serve.

Note: You would be amazed at how many students cut the fries and fried them right away after spending most of the class time socializing. Their fries were dark brown.

* * *

Working with Jim was fun yet again. We had to make stocks. First up was chicken stock. A basic recipe version is below:

CHICKEN STOCK

2 Raw chicken carcasses
Celery tops and leaves cut into 2-inch pieces
Carrots cut into 2-inch pieces
Onions cut into 2-inch pieces
Parsley bunch
Salt
Pepper
Put all ingredients in a stockpot and cover with water.
Bring to a boil and then reduce to a simmer for about 4 hours, partially covered.
Strain the stock.
Discard the bones and vegetables.

Making stock is not hard, just a bit time-consuming in the simmering process. It sounds easy enough. Strain it.

"Can you strain that stock?" I asked Jim.

"Sure. No problem." He replied and took the stock with him to the sink.

I didn't recall him taking another container. He could not be that oblivious, could he? I walked over. Jim was straining it right down the drain. I was fucking livid. What kind of idiot does something that stupid. You are making stock which means you want to keep it. Not strain it down the fucking drain!

"Are you kidding me?!" I screamed.

"You said to strain it…" he started to say

"In a container. Why the fuck are you still pouring it down the fucking drain? STOP!!! Jesus Christ! We spent four hours on it, and you pour it down the fucking drain?! Unfuckingbeleivable!" I was furious now. I was screaming at him. He started to cry. I didn't care.

He put the remaining stock down and walked away from me. Get the fuck out here, dumbass. How anyone could be that stupid is beyond me. Then again, it's Jim. The same Jim who cut his finger and still kept cutting vegetables with blood all over the board. I should have known better than to send a complete dullard to do a simple task of straining stock. The dumbass thought I wanted the carcass and vegetables? Oh, how tasty.

The Chef came over to me and was so pissed off I was shaking.

"What happened?" he asked

"That fucking idiot strained the stock down the fucking drain, and I am pissed," I replied.

"I can see that. However, you should not scold him like that." He replied

"How do you want me to scold him then? I can do better," I shot back.

"You can't berate people." He responded

"Some need it. Like Jim, for example. A simple thing of straining the stock. What does he do? He pours it down the fucking drain even though we said we would use it for other things. I can't escape idiots. I have them at work, and I have them here. Seriously, how do you do it every day without losing your mind?" I had to ask.

"You'll figure it out. Alcohol helps," answered Chef, and he laughed.

"Seriously, how do you do it? These people drive me crazy," I asked. I needed to know. The only thing stopping me from killing them is the jail time. I remembered the meme I saw. The older you get, the less a life sentence means. I get it. Retirement homes are $3,000 per month and more. Prison is free. No freedom. Hmmm, Decisions, decisions. If there is no body found, they are "missing."

***

I had an incident where I had to step in with a cook and a guest. The lady was looking at the pork Souvlaki while one of our 'cooks' was watching her. I was doing a quick line sweep.

"Excuse me. Are these beef or pork?" asked the guest. The sign clearly stated, "Pork Souvlaki" on the card above is attached to the sneeze guard. It's not entirely her fault. Guests are there to enjoy themselves and do not always read.

"Beef." Replied the cook on duty.

"Are you sure?" she asked

"Yes," he answered.

"Thank you." She replied and starting loading up her plate. Oh my God, really? Is this happening right now?

"Ma'am. Those are pork." I stated, stepping in.

"Are you sure?" she asked. Oh, was I getting the stink eye now from the cook. If looks could kill, I would be dead.

"Absolutely?" I replied. "It's a Greek dish and is made with pork."

"Excuse me! Those are beef!" snapped the cook. He was pissed, and there was malice in his tone. I overstepped my boundary to him, but I don't care.

"Do you want to do this now?" I snatched the sign off of the sneeze guard. "Do you see this?! Pork! P-O-R-K Pork! Look at that; it's in English too. If you are going to give out information, make sure you know what the Hell you are talking about and be accurate!"

"Ha! You should be sweeping the floors, not him. You don't know shit," said the patron to the cook. I was laughing. He was furious.

"Thanks for pointing that out. Pork is against my religion," said the guest thanking me.

"You are welcome," I replied and smiled at her. She walked away and went to the carvery area for some beef.

"I made those for over five years. You assholes think we are stupid. You condescend to us constantly because we came from another area. I have more experience in this than you. Get over yourself. Do you know how much shit you would have been in if that lady ate that and found out it was pork?" I asked him. He was silent. "Plenty." "You're welcome."

He remained silent and kept the dirty look on his face, and giving me the stink eye. There is nothing more fragile than an ego. I should have let him serve her that pork. I'm sure management would understand even though the item has a relatively large font. The customer is always right, and they would throw him under the bus to save face.

Let's look at the dish now—pork Souvlaki. These are on skewers, and in food service, they're marinated and grilled off. They are in some beef broth in the buffet to prevent them from drying out under the heat lamp. The souvlakis were garnished with green onions and feta cheese with pita bread right nearby.

These cooks were assholes. The constant holier-than-thou attitudes were annoying. The ass-kissing and trying to make me feel inferior to them was nothing short of annoying. I could see some felt threatened. I am sorry your façade is weak and easily crumbled. Oh, well. I will not lower my standards and keep quiet to stroke your ego and raise you're your standards.

* * *

I have listened to speakers on guest relations. One worked at Disney. At Disney, everyone picks up garbage. Nobody is too good that they can't pick up litter. I went to Disney in Florida and watched a gentleman in a suit with a Disney ID tag pick up trash off the sidewalk and place it in the receptacle.

Another thing I learned at the seminar was you could not get frustrated with the guest, although sometimes you do, and it is tough not to, especially when they are rude and belligerent. At Disney, all staff is always in character in public areas. We saw this first hand. We went back to the Magic Kingdom at night for the Haunted Mansion. We were looking around for the entrance. We approached two young men in suits near the cemetery.

"Excuse me, " asked my spouse. "we are looking for the Haunted Mansion.

"Does this not look like the Haunted Mansion?" replied one of the young men without changing his mortuary worker pose and his expression on his face. He did not even crack a smile. He stayed very straight face. He had a professional accent while doing so of that of a mortician.

"Thank you," replied my spouse. We walked further away. "What an ass."

"No, he wasn't. He stayed in character. Those guys are dressed like morticians and have to stay in character at all times." I replied. "Try and get one to break character."

"Okay, I will,"

It was fun watching them try. Disney staff is too good. I will compare them to soldiers at Buckingham Palace.

The Disney speaker said it is easier to assume they left their brains in the car or coat check. It's a fun place, and they are overwhelmed with everything around them that they are not looking for the everyday things like toilets, escalators, elevators. They are thinking about things like rides and shows. I missed the restroom sign in front of me at a Las Vegas casino. I can validate that.

Plus, when I went to Disney, I struggled to find the entrance to a ride with my niece and nephew. They were young children under ten at the time, so they wanted to go on the ride—no time to pull out the map with excited children dragging you. I'm not stupid; I was distracted and occupied with two children. Parents can have this in a department store.

Another thing I learned is the guest will only listen to the first thing you say to them, so make it count. I had a coworker who showed me this. We were standing in front of an escalator. We watched a couple of younger males in their twenties coming our way, and they seemed lost.

"They are looking how to get upstairs. These boys will listen to the first thing I tell them. Watch this," she said to me in a low voice. They came over as she said they would.

"Excuse me, ma'am. How do we get upstairs?" asked one of the young men.

"Well, I will give you three options. You can take the elevator at the end of the floor down this aisle, or you can jump high, or you can use the escalator behind me," she replied. They chuckled.

"Thank you," he replied and took his friends to the other end of the floor down the aisle to the elevator.

"Wow," I said in shock. I was amazed at the same time. She called it.

"It's not just guests either. You can do that to just about anyone. They only listen to the first thing you say. It's true of anyone who wants an argument. You'll be lucky if they listen at all. They are too busy thinking of the next thing they are going to say. Have a debate with someone. They are usually misinformed and will run with stupid stuff. So make your comments count. Get the most crucial thing out first.," she informed me. She is right.

Chapter 4

Working full-time midnights and going to school was rough. I even picked up afternoon shifts on the weekends. One day on the afternoon shift, something I ate was not sitting. I am so glad I was working alone. Here is another chance for you to laugh at me. I was in a clearing area for the buffet. I could feel my stomach churn—painful jabs in my lower abdomen. I let one out. Silent but deadly. Oh my God, did it stink? When the skunk is gagging, you know it is terrible. A garbage dump is mild in comparison. I quickly left the area.

I came back about 20 minutes later. There were a group of servers in the serving aisle. I casually walked up to check the glass racks and switch them out for new ones. I cleared the plates while they were chatting.

"Hey, did you happen to notice an odour coming from the flood drain?" one asked me. We will call her Lisa.

"No. I haven't," I was dying. It's hilarious. The servers think it's the drain. Talk about some serious hang time. Oh my god. It's like it sticks to the walls—toxic ass leak. Farts are the lowest form of comedy. So what? Inside I am dying. Would you admit to that? I didn't think so. I kept it up all night. Now it was a game.

"Well, keep a watch. I think the drain is backing up," Lisa replied, pointing to the drain on the floor.

I let them carry on and felt the urge in my gut again. I held it back until the servers all left the area and released it. Another sneaker. Silent but deadly. I immediately left the room.

I don't know what I had. I think it was a combination of cabbage rolls and egg salad. Who could be sure? If I were to give out this toxic recipe, I know it would be heavily shared on social media. A How-to Guide to getting revenge on your coworkers. Would you please not use this combination-lethal. I think it goes against the Geneva Convention. Biological warfare. I left for my standard 20 minutes to come back and find someone from maintenance checking the drains. OMG, I am dying now.

I did acting classes, and let me tell you, and they came in handy now. Anyone else would have pissed their pants and broke out in laughter. Not me. I walked over to the station like nothing was amiss. I was oblivious and had no idea. Right?

"Hey, did you notice any odours coming from this area earlier?" asked the maintenance guy.

"Nope. Nothing out of the ordinary. Coffee, Soda, Tea, and warm beer. What's up?" I asked with as much sincerity as I could muster.

"The servers are complaining about a possible sewer backup. I can't see anything. Nothing is coming up, or there would be remnants on the floor." He started. He shined his flashlight in the drain. "Nope. Nothing"

"I'll keep a watch for you," I replied.

"Thank you." He replied and left the area.

Maintenance got called to address the backup again. OMG, now this is hilarious. I felt that churning in my guts again and let it sneak out. Pfffffttttttttt. It went for about five seconds. The spoils of war going on in my colon. Yes, I left immediately.

I remember how I had a protein shake too. Protein shakes, egg salad, and cabbage rolls are lethal. Oh no. My ass is toxic. In a way, I was hoping nobody would notice. In another way, I was enjoying the entertainment. It is also known as crop dusting when you Fart and walk at the same time. In my case, it was drop and f=go but close enough. It is still vile but entertaining at the same time.

I was leaving, Lisa was heading back to the station. She was busy talking and didn't notice my exit. That was close. She went into the area and wait for it.

"Oh my god!" she exclaimed. And there it is—the prize winner with serious hang time. Yes, I was enjoying this now. Forget the raging battle in my colon and the gas pains that went with it. It is too funny.

I could not resist. I had to go back. I waited and grabbed an empty glass rack I could find. I had to hear this. I filled up the glass racks six high on the transport and went back to the scene of the crime. I casually pushed the glass racks in and placed them in the storage area.

"Hey, did you notice anything?" asked Lisa.

"No. What's up?" I asked innocently.

"I don't know what it is but every half hour or so, as soon as I walk in, it's like 'Whoosh" the smell comes from this drain. It's disgusting." She explained.

"I don't know. I am here for like 5 minutes at a time, so I didn't notice," I explained, trying to cover my tracks in my calmest and most innocent voice.

"It's horrible!" she cried.

"Again, I don't smell anything. I don't know what to tell you," I lied. Don't judge me. Would you admit to this? I didn't think so. I am in too deep now. I felt the rumbling again. Oh shit. This one will give me away. Luckily there was another door. I slipped out and let it close behind. Pfffffffffftttttttttttttttt. I let it go and exited the empty hall. I'm sure someone walked into it like a brick wall. I was not hanging around. Seriously, what the Hell is wrong with my ass tonight?

Maintenance got called yet again. Maintenance was rechecking the drain and saw me coming. He got up off his knees from shining the light in the gutter. In a larger building, the drains are more significant and have drain covers over them.

"There is nothing wrong with the drains. I have been here four times. I found nothing each time. I will bet someone is farting. I'll bet it is one of the girls. It was so bad they smelled it at the other end of the bar, and it's twenty feet away! That's impressive!" he reported.

"Wow?" I asked. I was going to burst. It was Pure entertainment and 15/10 embarrassment. I can't let anyone know, but oh my God, this is hilarious. I just let it die. Whenever I had to let out a toxic bomb, I made sure no one was near me. I cop dusted other areas and usually walking between stations. I will never mix that combination again.

It gets worse. We rode a bus to work from a central parking lot. I had to get on a bus with several other employees. They were air-conditioned and the windows up. Oh no. Please no. I was sitting with one of my friends, and here comes the rumbling again in my gut. It was only 3 miles, but here it goes. Pffffttttttttttttt.

I elbowed her and whispered, "shut up. Don't say a word,"

She was burying her nose in her sleeve and trying not to make it obvious. She was trying not to gag. I knew she was secretly cursing me as the silent but deadly cloud wafted around the bus. It is pure entertainment to see everyone blaming each other for it.

"Who farted? My God, I would lay claims to that. That is impressive. The whole bus is gagging." Claimed a coworker.

The bus came to a stop and opened. There was a bit of a rush to get off and exhale. Most had their noses in their shirts. Offensively, they would rather smell their body odours after 8 hours than my stinky farts, but I get it. I was gagging too.

"You're an asshole. Do not ever eat what you had again. That is simply wrong." said my friend when we were out of hearing distance from the rest of our coworkers. It's one for the books.

Chapter 5

I got to work on the line assisting the cooks. I was amazed at how little some of them knew. I witnessed one trying to convince a customer a thigh was a breast in fried chicken. I had to step in. I had five years of experience with fried chicken at this time.

"May I?" I asked.

"What?" he asked and was annoyed by my interruption.

"I have done chicken for over five years." I picked up the tongs and flipped over the piece I knew was a chicken breast.

"Look for the ribs. When you see ribs, it is chicken breast—white meat." I then grabbed a thigh. "Look at the end. There is always a little nob of fat. That is how you can tell it is a thigh. Dark meat."

I grabbed the centre breast and flipped it over. "This piece is the centre breast." The cook was annoyed now. It wasn't long before I was the subject of being a know-it-all. Yeah, I made a new friend. It was better the customer was happy she got what she wanted. Someone's pride is the most fragile thing on Earth.

He kept shooting me dirty looks, and I finally could not take it anymore. I walked right over to him. "Do you have a minute?" I asked.

"What do you want?" he asked with malice in his voice.

"I get you are mad at me, but you clearly can't tell the difference between a breast and a thigh. I feel sorry for your girlfriend. Yeah. I heard everything you said about me and what a know-it-all asshole I am, so I might as well embrace the asshole. I would rather be a know-it-all than a complete dumbass like you. Yeah, and you even tried to convince a guest that Pork Souvlaki was beef. It's in the name Pork Souvlaki." I smiled at him

"Here, want to rub my thigh? I asked, rubbing my chest. I smirked at him. He was more pissed now and didn't care. I'm sorry you are oblivious. Ever get fried chicken before? Seriously. If you are going to do a job, have some fucking knowledge on it. I walked away. I know he had plenty more to say about me behind my back, of course. This trend would continue.

The cooks started to mistreat me even more, but I was not taking their shit. They would dump an entire hotel pan of chits in front of the floor blower after I mopped the floor and then snap their fingers at me like some little bitch servant to clean it up. I outright refused.

"Clean it up!" one yelled.

"Fuck you! You're the one who made the mess, and you clean it up. I am not your fucking maid!" I shouted back.

"Clean it up now!"

"NO! Fuck You!" I shouted back. I grabbed the broom and handed it to him. "YOU DUMPED IT ON PURPOSE! YOU FUCKING DO IT!" I screamed right in his face. I always get a kick out of the assholes who think that the louder they scream, the more in the right they think they are.

The Dunning-Kruger effect shows that the more knowledge you lack, the more bad decisions and mistakes you will make. They also lack the wisdom to know they are doing it wrong. Also, let's add that the louder someone yells, the more they realize they are wrong. It is about deflection and arrogance.

"You're the steward. You do it!" he shouted back.

"You have no authority, and you can fuck right off, asshole!" I shouted back at him and had my finger in his face.

The Sous Chef came over. "What's going on here?" he asked.

"This asshole deliberately dumped a whole hotel pan of chits in front of the fan on a wet floor, and he expects me to be his birch and clean it up. It ain't happening."

"Just clean it up." Said the sous chef

"Hell no. I won't do it. That asshole deliberately made the mess so that asshole can clean it."

"Are you refusing to follow a direct order?" he asked, trying to push his authority on me. I didn't have it.

"You're damn right. Do you want to get Human Resources? There are cameras, and I'm going to win. Bring it on!" I stated and glared him right in the eyes. When I am right, I don't back down.

"I'm calling your supervisor." He stated.

"Want me to dial it?" I shot back. There is no way in Hell I am backing down from this one.

"I'm right here, " said a voice coming up behind me.

"Good, you talk. It's my break time." I walked away from them. They can fight it out. I am not cleaning up after that asshole. Case closed. And for the record, I didn't have to. The asshole got the write-up. Not me. They got someone else to clean it up. If I were his sous chef, that asshole would be on his knees with a scraper peeling the wet paper off the floor. Yeah, I made another friend.

* * *

Some of these assholes would burn deliberately burn pans and expect me to clean them and that and the fine cooking skills they do not possess. Nope. There was a policy for it, and they had to clean it. Not me. When you have enemies, make sure you are more informed than they are. This behaviour went on for a while. I never backed down. When you are in the right, never give an inch of ground.

The head chef was an ass. He looked down on his stewards like they were garbage. He shook hands with his cooks on his last day and skipped over everyone in my department, even though we worked for him. The cooks kissed his ass to the point where it was revolting: blatant ass-kissing and brown-nosing. It was disgusting to watch.

I talked to him about the prospect of the opportunity to cook and advance. I don't kiss ass. I was interested in the bakery. He had me bake him a cake. I did and brought it to him the next day. It was a layered banana pecan cake with buttercream icing. I even decorated it with Candied Pecans. I placed it in the fridge in the bakery for him with a note saying it was his.

I later found out one of the bakers left it out near the oven where it melted all over the table, and of course, he had lots to Saay about it. Every juvenile insult and tantrum from a grown-ass man. Wow, they are a bunch of spoiled babies and easily threatened. I have many friends in the building, and of course, they told me all about it. I was pissed off, yes—however, all good things to those who wait. I will bide my time.

When it was the turd's last day, the cooks bought him all kinds of gifts. They loved him so much. Now let the truth be told. Here's how much he appreciated them and appreciated the gifts he received. He opened them and ordered my supervisor to put them in the garbage compacter. He did not take a single thing with him. I got the duty of disposing of them and was sworn to secrecy never to tell them. I don't work there anymore, so here it is. Most still had the cellophane on them. Your idle was nothing more than an ignorant bitch, and now you know how much he thought of you. Shit, he scrapes off his shoes. Your gifts and ass-kissing were appreciated so much, and it went straight to the garbage. Cheers.

On another note, this insufferable cunt told me to my face that I would never be given an opportunity in any kitchen as long as he was around. I was close to completing my culinary program, and I was ready to challenge him with Human Resources. The piece of shit left before I could put it in action. We got rid of an abusive ass once before. I signed his card with the following: "Thank you for all of your encouragement. I got a 4.0 in my culinary program. Thank you."

I had no respect for that twat. It was a well-disguised 'fuck you." I hope he got it, but I will bet it was discarded in the nearest receptacle like his precious gifts without even looking at it.

* * *

In that class, students didn't do things properly. We had one who would spend 20 minutes on a garnish of a fruit or vegetable carving to present her food.

"Is this practical in the real world?" I asked.

"Yes, it is," she shot back in a snotty tone.

"Oh, it is? Is it? How many times have you gotten fucking shit like that on your plate at any restaurant? How many?!" I let her have it. She was my lab partner and wasted more time than I care to count by doing stupid shit like that. Garnish takes 2 seconds, tops.

The Chef came over and shook his head. "People want to eat now. If you're going to make sculptures, you should have to an art class," he flat out told her. "You are wasting time, and food is getting cold. Garnish is quick. It should be no more than a couple of seconds."

As soon as he was gone, I could not resist it. "Is there an echo? Oh wow. Now move your fucking ass," I shot at her. I was utterly disgusted and appalled at how full of excuses and shit she was.

In another class, she was too busy talking and on her phone. She missed the deadline to turn in her dish and blamed the oven. She set the oven to 400 F. She took the time to put the thermometer in it for probing meat on a silicone cord. It read 382 F . She tried to blame the oven and 18 F for why she couldn't get her dish done on time.

 Again, 18 F would extend it another five or six minutes maximum. Excuses, excuses. How about shut up and get your work done? Nope, it is always someone else's fault, or something was not working right. She had to wait for someone or any other excuse she could make up. The only thing consistent with her was a delay and constant excuses. She failed the class. Does it come as a shock to you? Not me either. Excuses seriously piss me off.

It amazes me how many students will skip mandatory classes and wonder why they fail the course. Nutrition class sucked. I was not too fond of it, but I finished it. It was my lowest mark. Most of the ones who didn't complete the program were because of this one or the English class and not showing up. Show up and make an effort. It makes a difference.

I excelled at the food costing. As a chef, this is where the money is—your controls. Control your costs, and you control your profits. It is the basic rule of the 30s. Your essential costs are 30% Food costs, 30% Labour Costs, 30 % Rent/ Utilities, and 10% profit in food and beverage. Without understanding these calculations and controls, hand in your keys now and save yourself the embarrassment.

So a simple pub with a bacon cheeseburger deluxe with fries.

Bun	$ 0.50
Cheese	$0.50
Lettuce	$0.08
Onion slice	$0.05
Tomato slice	$0.10
Bacon (2)	$0.40
6 Oz beef	$1.49
Mayo	$0.10
Mustard	$0.03
Ketchup	$0.03
Fries	$0.20
Napkin	$0.03
Total	$ 3.51

Take your $3.51 costs and divide by 30% gives you a selling price of $ 11.70, so rounding it to $ 11.95 menu price.

Beverage costs are generally under 20%, with soda having an excellent profit margin. Your service persons are your salespeople. You want them to sell gravy, usually at least another $1.00 and costs like $0.09 in food costs.

Alcohol sales are a great way to get the sales bill up. The average person will consume an average of 2 beers in a dine-in situation. Now that bill goes to $20.95, and if the server is timely, they can suggest a dessert where 60 % on average will take it, so let's add another $6 to a total of $26.95. A modest tip rate of 15% leaves a $4.05 tip, whereas just the burger, fries, and water might get them $1.80.

Another suggestion in the service is not to let that beer go dry. If it goes dry, your odds of making that sale on a second beer drop drastically when you are offering a second beer when between 1/3 and 1/4 of the beverage remaining will have a much higher chance of a refill. Why? A couple of reasons. You feel you are not getting the proper attention and want to leave. It's empty. It means you are done. However, having the offer before it goes empty makes you feel more welcome, and there is a higher probability of you staying and, of course, spending more.

In culinary school, we went to a couple of food plants. It just blows my mind that there are people who have no idea where food originates. If there is a shortage of something like eggs, chicken wings, you will hear comments like, "Why don't they just go to the store?"

The mentality is just ignorance and living in oblivious fantasy land. Fish come from lakes, streams, oceans and farms. Hens lay one egg. Chickens have two legs, two wings, two thighs and two breasts cut into three. We covered this already. Chickens only grow so fast before they are ready for the slaughterhouse like any other livestock.

Food preparation is not pretty. Animals are slaughtered. Fish are filleted. It's pretty gruesome, but if you like that steak, fried chicken and fish and chips, it's a fact of life. Ever watch a cheetah take down a zebra on the National Geographic channel? Food.

In part of the program, we had to serve Lobster Americaine. With that dish, a live lobster is cut in half then done in a pan. We stabbed it in the head through the brain before slicing it down the body to cut it in half. Again, food preparation is not pretty.

Farmers grow crops like corn, wheat, tomatoes, apples and other fruits and vegetables. They are harvested and then brought to the market or a food processing plant to be canned or made into other products, then they are shipped to the market.

We already saw that hoarding could cause shortages and did during that Covid-19 nightmare. Hoarding toilet paper by the skid, hand sanitizer to gouge people online. It caused shortages. It brought out the worst in some people. We can all agree on that.

In culinary school, you have to make things you don't like. It's the way it goes in food service. I think liver is vile, but you have to make it for them if someone wants it. We had a class where we had to make breaded liver where an entire cow liver was on the table. You had to cut your liver steak out of it and cook it for the Chef to grade. Sweetbreads were on the menu as well.

Sweetbreads are the thymus from the throat or neck of the calf or lamb. It can be the ovaries or testicles as well. It is soaked in saltwater and then poached in milk. 80% of the class did not show up for the day we made them.

"This is the day we find out how good of a liar you are?" smirked the Chef. "I know some of you find these disgusting, like those who are missing in action. There will be no make-up for them. They are getting a zero. I will ask you how it tastes, and there better be a piece missing, or you are eating it in front of me. As I said, we will see how well you lie."

I had Vicks under my nose. I wouldn't say I like liver and the odour it makes while it cooks. It's pretty disgusting. I made it as per the recipe and cut a small piece out of it. I immediately tossed it in the garbage.

In the class, we had to taste our food regularly. Plates were graded on presentation, seasoning, taste, garnish and temperature. The things you would expect at a restaurant. Do you want cold food? Do you want a trainwreck on your plate? Do you want overcooked, overly salty slop?

I brought mine up well garnished and hot. I walked with confidence. I placed it in front of the Chef and smiled. "Bon Appetite."

"Did you taste it?' he asked.

"Of course. It was great. It is something I can truly say that I am proud to serve you. I hope you enjoy it just as much as I did," I replied straight-faced.

"Okay then. I will be the judge of that." He replied before taking a bite. I was waiting. That was pure bullshit I spewed. Maybe I laid it on a little too thick.

"Very well done. I think you should take another bite, though," Chef said, looking at me with a smile.

"But I made it just for you, and it is not appropriate to eat off of a customer's plate," I insisted.

"Good answer. I believe you but perhaps not as much on selling it to me. You are not a bad liar." He said, smiling at me. "I'm giving you a 9/10. When you lie to me, don't overdo it."

"Thank you, Chef," I replied and took away the rest of the plate.

When the sweetbreads went up, I can assure you I played it cool with less embellishment. I got a 10/10. I will bet if I did a Joey acting lesson of rubbing my stomach and saying "mmmm," it would have got me a mouthful of that nasty stuff.

If you have ever watched cooking shows, you will know that those things happen where someone gets served raw chicken. When you have a meat thermometer on your sleeve and still manage to fuck that up, you deserve that zero you got. It is nothing short of not giving a shit or laziness. Take your pick. It is still pathetic no matter what way you slice it.

I am amazed at the participation ribbon generation. These people always look for half marks or some praise no matter how terrible their job is. You burnt my steak, but you want a compliment on your efforts with the French fries. It doesn't work that way. You ruined the central part of my meal, don't come to me fishing for a compliment. I'm pissed off, and I certainly will not be trying to make you feel better and stroke your ego or blow smoke up your ass telling you that you did a good job. You didn't. It's fucking shit. That is what I will say to you.

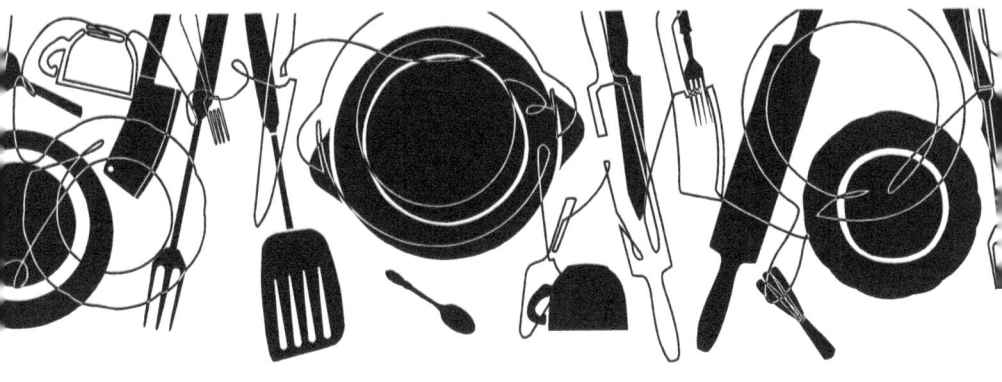

Chapter 6

The new Chef came, and he was very nice. I was scrubbing a pan in our high-end restaurant. He came over to shake my hand. My hands were covered in all kinds of leftovers from my pot sink. I rinsed my hands off under the faucet and frantically dried them on my pants.

"Don't worry about that. In this job we get dirty. I am used to it," Chef said, extending his hand. Wow. He is a genuine guy. He respects people. I was excited. Positive changes are coming. I, of course, gladly accepted his hand. He instantly got my respect and still has it to this day.

Within a few weeks, a job posting went up, and I applied. I got it. I was so happy, grateful and excited all at the same time. Someone gave me a shot. When someone gives you something, always accept it with gratitude.

The other thing is when your mentor is willing to roll up their sleeves and get dirty right next to you. That is the way I am. I have never been too good to wash dishes. I have had dishwashers I adored. They were hardworking and stepped up. I like to run my ship like a family. Everyone is important and a link in the chain. We have all connected and work together like a well-oiled chain.

I had dishwashers come right in without dinner, and staff chipped in to buy him a meal. I occasionally buy my guys and girls drinks at the end of the shift. I have stepped up and made my staff meals on busy nights, so they had a nice dinner. It is my way of saying "Thank you," and I appreciate you. There is an unwritten rule in the kitchen where you do not make your staff food. I say fuck that. If you're busy, I have no problem making it for you.

I had chefs I worked for making me food when I was in the weeds, and I can tell you whatever they made was greatly appreciated because it came with appreciation and respect. I do it when I can. My mentor chefs fed me all kinds of things to expand my knowledge and palate. I loved to learn and try new things.

I always love it when we can critique and make it better. As a team, we all have the unique gifts we bring to the table. I love soul food. My favourite. BBQ Southern cuisine. My other favourites are Asian and Italian cuisine because I love them so much. When I make a special dinner at home, it's one of those, depending on the seasons. Summer and fall, I love to make soul food. The rest of the year, I love Asian and Italian for entertaining.

I also love Scottish comfort food as it is part of my ancestry: bangers and mash, meat pies, mince n tatties, and good pub food. My grandfather made the best meat pies, hands down. When I get an excellent Scottish pie, it makes me think of the old two-story house he had. He had a lot of property, and I loved visiting him. It's funny how food can bring back happy memories of dinner with grandpa at the old house.

We would sit at the old metal frame table with the heavy metal padded chairs and eat his meat pies. They were amazing. He had a large kitchen, and we spent a lot of time there. We were sitting around the table while he made us old-school Scottish food. He was a good cook and loved making things for us. It was always made with love, and he always made us little pies of our own and had extra gravy for them. His bangers and mash were the best. It's my grandpa, of course. They were the best, just like your Nona's spaghetti. Nobody makes it better than Nona.

I can still remember that kitchen. Unfortunately, the house was old and got torn down after he passed. He had a large window over his sink. A half-wall separated the kitchen from the dining room with a decorative tiered shelf on top of nicknacks and other décor items.

I was very young when he died, but those pies still bring it back when I eat them. My brother and cousins said I am starting to look like him as I get older. That is a massive compliment to me. He was awesome. He was tall like me, and he was fun and caring. I am good with it.

* * *

I applied for the job, and I got it. Those rude, daft cooks were butt-hurt. Temper tantrums are comparable. Immediately after, I was allowed to pick where I could go in the resort. I went to the buffet where my friends were, and of course, I had enemies there too. I had them everywhere. Stand up for yourself, and you are an asshole.

I put up with all kinds of childish behaviour and outright bullying from them. Stomping on clean floors after they walk through flour right in customer areas, pots and pans melted to the plastic carts, pots full of burnt and caked-on slop, and so on. It was very evident in the lack of skill some of these people had. The inability to identify a standard nine-cut chicken was a good indicator. The hilarious part is they think they can still condescend to me.

I had co-workers refuse to train me or even assist in any way. There is nothing worse than a sore loser. They left their stations jacked with dirty dishes, improperly stocked or empty altogether. There was an excuse for everything. Weak managers continued to let it slide.

Let's start with the lady that worked in the staff cafeteria. Her setup was all about making tips and minimal work. I timed her to make a sandwich on my break. Six Minutes!! Lunches are half an hour, and at that rate, she serves six people. That sixth person has to wolf it down so fast they are going to choke. The others go without. I don't think she ever broke a sweat on that line. That area was fast when I started like ten years ago. Now it is so relaxed you can't get served if you are more than the sixth person. Pathetic.

"Oh, sweetheart, would you like bacon? Would you like tomatoes? Would you like lettuce. "Oh, sweetheart, would you like fries?" Anything to drag the process out and do less work. Oh, sweetheart, I am going to vomit and lose my shit.

It is funny when I started 12 years ago that the person doing it could serve 20 people when it took her the same time to do 4. Is it a surprise that it closed and replaced with vending machines and grab-and-go sandwiches?

In the buffet, I got to see the sculpture creations raise it's ugly heads once again. They are wasting time making hideous sculptures to place in chafing dishes and on serving platters. It does not look good. It looks like shit. My Chef reminded them. He was a great guy and showed me more things.

One of the funniest moments I had with him was when I was at the dessert station. There was a chocolate and raspberry mousse that stood out. The Chef came over.

"Did you you try this? He asked.

"Yes"

"What did you think of it?" he asked.

"I thought it was a little flat and could use a little more flavour," I replied.

"How very nice and professional of you. It tastes like fucking shit now; get rid of it." He replied.

I went and grabbed the bowl as assigned and took it towards the garbage.

"Stop," commanded the Chef. "Taste it again." I stopped and tasted it as he asked.

"Now, how does it taste?" he asked.

"It tastes like fucking shit, Chef," I replied.

"Aah, there's hope for you yet," he said, smiling at me and walked away. I started laughing. That was hilarious. I still laugh whenever I tell that.

I tossed that shit as instructed. I still use that phrase. There is no other way to describe substandard food. It tastes like fucking shit. I used this a lot over my years of experience. Some of the "creativity" out there is something to be desire. It is the art of bastardizing the classics to try and make a name for yourself. It worked. You did, but not in a positive way.

I had another co-worker who used one of the funniest things on this Chef. She felt she was given too many tasks and asked, "Ad while we are it, Why don't we just jam a broomstick up my ass so I can sweep the floor as I go?" He did not deserve it but handled it like a pro.

"I am not even going to respond to that shit," was his response, and he walked away—an actual class act. I loved working for him.

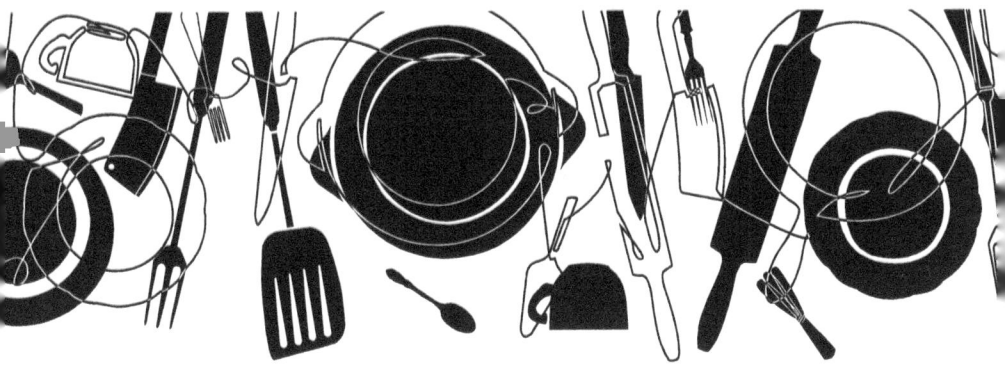

Chapter 7

It wasn't long before it was time for the annual Battle of the Hors D'oevres. It is a city-wide competition that benefits Big Brother & Big Sisters. I love to compete. I worked with a chef on the side while doing culinary school, and we did a couple of these style events. One was at a window plant for their 50th anniversary. There were several restaurants at the event. Winning feels awesome. I wanted to take on some of these arrogant assholes that treated me like shit when I was in dishwashing and hopefully kick a little ass.

A few of us were allowed to move up from dishwashing, and of course, they were treated like dirt as well. I had the desire to knock the arrogant ones down a few pegs, and I was going to take pleasure in it.

I signed up, and within a few hours, I heard the comments come back. "Who the fuck does he think he is?" "I'm going to put that asshole in his place." "Beating that arrogant know-it-all is going to be fun." "I can't wait to see him cry like a bitch." "That fucking faggot is going to learn how much he sucks." These are just some of the examples I heard. Yeah, I made some friends.

I decided to do a fusion dish. I used eggroll wraps and filled them with diced chicken, julienne carrots, celery, daikon radish, hoisin sauce, onion, Asian cabbage and carrots. The eggrolls were served with a wasabi buttermilk ranch dressing on the side.

Now my competition. Bob, the same guy who dumped the chits on the wet floor in front of the fan, did slices of beef on skipping stones with black lava rock. It was very monochromatic and was devoid of garnish as well. It was a very dull presentation. I tried the beef, and of course, it was overcooked and chewy. I have made Japanese beef before. It is served rare to medium-rare at the most with nice traces of red in the meat itself. He called it Kobe Beef. I was trying hard not to laugh.

Kobe Beef is the most expensive beef you can buy and a real delicacy. It is a strain of Japanese Black cattle. Kobe beef is to be prepared with great care, unlike this hack. He is also the same person who showed me that putting something disgusting on a pizza deters guests from eating it and less work for him—way to go, Chef. A waste of food. Shameful.

Now entry number two. A deep-fried olive called Olive fun, and it was served with bottled barbecue sauce. He did it as a joke, but it was a fuck you and the disrespect shined through the presentation quite well. I tried it for fun, and it was nothing short of revolting.

Another, Neil, decided to do a bland dish in flavour but had some lovely edible flowers on the plate. I will give credit to the presentation. At the serving time, we had to describe our dishes to the three judges who were picked from other areas, including Human Resources and front-of-house management.

The results were in. I won. The ensuing tantrums began. Neil and Bob stormed out and didn't even clean their mess. The bitched and moaned and carried on like children. It was embarrassing to watch. Like overcooked beef on a monochrome display looked remotely appetizing. Then there are Neil's flowers with shitty food served with it. Olive fun? Please. They had no sportsmanship in them whatsoever. They got beat by a former dishwasher whom they used to look down upon and spit on. Welcome to Hell. On a personal note, I went with the names Neil and Bob because they are conniving cocksuckers.

* * *

It came time to try and get a team together. As you probably guessed, none of the previous cooks wanted to help. I recruited from the new hires. They were glad to help out and had not yet been negatively influenced by that environment. We will touch on some of that later.

I had a couple of the cooks come up to me and congratulate me on the in-house victory, but they all stopped offering assistance from there. There is nothing worse than a sore loser. It is a toxic environment, but when they have to go and poison the atmosphere further, their fragile, little ego got crushed. The ego is the most fragile thing in the world.

"Good for you beating them. Now they can kiss your ass," said one cook. She smiled and gave me a thumbs up.

"Thank you. And yes, they can kiss my ass—sore losers." I replied.

We put in extra hours to get the team battle-ready. A few modifications had to been made to the appetizer. We breaded the wonton wrap against what I had initially wanted, but upper management wanted to help. They wanted to ensure victory. I felt it was enough, but a drop of sweet and sour was added to my wasabi ranch dressing for a bit of colour. I used two small dots on the creamy green hue to add contrast.

I found out Neil and Bob joined their friend's restaurant to go against me in the finals. Now that is a sore loser at its finest. You go against your employer to try and save your vanity. That is just brazen insolence. They showed off their concept and came up with the outside restaurant that is no longer in business. It had a brief run.

I was up against pretty flowers and overcooked, chewy and dry beef, so I am sure their skills will be influenced. I graduated in the top 10% of my class and was clearly up against no class. I was looking forward to it.

*　*　*

Our old Chef came to visit during the battle preparation and saw me wearing a white chef's jacket. I heard him ask "Who's that?" to one of the sous chefs. I could feel my back going up. I despise that asshole.

He came over and held his hand out for me to shake it. I shoved my hands deep in my pants pockets and gave him a dirty look. Sorry, it is an involuntary reaction when I see someone I can't stand and have no respect for them.

"I wasn't good enough to shake it before when I was a dishwasher. I sure as hell am not shaking it now. You told me I would never make it while you were here. Well, let me tell you, I won the battle of the Hors D'Oeurves and beat out you ass kissers. Now I go to the city-wide competition. It's reasons like this why you shouldn't judge people. I have a team to prep. Please excuse me." Yeah, that was rude but ultimately called deserved. When someone offers you their hand, you should take it. When you don't, it says a lot. Now he knows, and you would believe how good that felt. The look of shock on the sous chef's face was priceless. I will not shake the hand of a disrespectful twat.

I did get spoken to about my behaviour towards the former Chef. However, they knew what had previously happened. But I was told when someone offers you their hand to shake, I should accept it. Sure, but not from someone who has disrespected me before. Not because of who I was but the colour of the shirt that I wore in my job. He skipped over some of my co-workers because of the same reason. That makes you an insufferable cunt. For this, I have no respect. I would not offer my hand to him if covered in snot or other bodily excretions.

* * *

The competition night was a bit scary. I had to lead my team, and we worked our asses off. We deserved this win. With that other team made up of the butt-hurt sore losers, I wanted that victory. I wanted it so bad I could taste it.

We showed up at the large banquet facility. They didn't have a deep fryer ready for me. I was getting anxious to the point that if they dragged it out much longer, I would vomit. I was given a deep fryer, but of course, it needed cleaning. I was pointed in the direction of where the oil and soap were. I assembled my team of 4. There were three new hires and me as well as our Sous Chef Ann. I love this lady to death, and we are still friends.

I took Ken with me on the fryer, Alex on dressing, Andre on Sweet and sour sauce and Ann finished the tray with her carved vegetable garnished. I was cooking, Ken plated. We used disposable bamboo bowls and 2 oz cups to make it environmentally friendly. The Hors D'ouevres were served on platters with banana leaves. That was the first time I ever used those. A quick sear on the charbroiler to make them bright green is all it takes.

The presentation looked terrific—the bright green platters with our little bamboo boats and eggrolls with wasabi ranch dressing. I was very proud of what we accomplished. They announced our team, and the banquet servers took our trays out. We all nodded at each other. We got this. They were hot, the presentation rocked, and so does the taste.

One of the banquet chefs came in. He walked right over to me. He probably could smell my nervousness from across the giant kitchen. "They love it. I just had to let you know. You can relax. It's up to the judges to vote Critics Choice and the attendees to vote for People's Choice. You did well. Relax and enjoy the night. No matter what happens, you did well and should be proud." He said and shook my hand.

The anticipation was killing me. Team Butt-Hurt went next. I smiled at them. It was a fuck you, but a smile is all it takes sometimes. Kill with kindness with just the right amount of malice in the mix. They deserve to lose again, and I can't wait to see their faces when they do. It made me smile. There is nothing like kicking someone's ass twice. It makes you feel warm and tingly all over.

"We now ask all teams to line up behind your captains and will be going out in order of service," said one of the organizers, projecting his voice for everyone to hear in the large kitchen. My crew was ready.

Our dish was used to announce us as we entered the hall. "Fowl Mouth Fury" I never said how the name came about. It's a play on words. Chefs swear, and it is a chicken dish. Fowl Mouth. The fury comes from the wasabi. We got loud applause as soon as we walked into the hall. They loved it. I was honoured. I was already a winner as far as I was concerned, and so was my team.

We lined up across the front of the banquet hall in our prospective teams and waited for the judges to announce the winners. I looked over and saw our head Chef in the front row. I smiled and nodded at him. He smiled back. He then looked over to where Neil and Bob were. He was no longer smiling. You could see the look of disgust he gave them. He was not amused by this behaviour at all. He snapped a few photos with his cell phone.

"Before we announce the winners, we want to thank each team for a job well done. The guests enjoyed them all." Said one of the judges and got another round of applause from the guests.

"Thank you. And now for the People's Choice. Fowl Mouth Fury!" the audience roared. I was in heaven. I walked over with my team and gladly accepted the medal and the People's Choice award. I can't even remember who won Critics Choice, but I later found out we missed it by one point because one of the judges didn't think the eggroll was cooked thoroughly. This judge was not a food professional, and it showed. The inside contents were precooked before being wrapped in the eggroll. The eggroll was flash-fried, then breaded and fried again. So, yes, it was most certainly cooked thoroughly.

In the end, I don't give a shit. I got an award, and team butt-hurt did not. You could see the sour defeat on Bob's and Neil's faces. That was better than the Critic's Choice to me—double the arrogance and twice the fall.

I bought my team pitchers of beer, and they had food for us at the bar. Neil and Bob came over to our table later that night. We were happy. So I assumed to try and discount the win and piss on our party in pure sore loser fashion.

"Do you have a minute?" asked Neil.

"Sure." I got up from the table and excused myself.

"Congratulations on your win," he said. You could tell he didn't mean a word of it, and I was waiting for the 'but' part.

"Thank you," I replied to be professional.

"You don't deserve it, though." He continued. And here it is.

"I beg to differ. The people have spoken, and yours was not awarded just like the last time. Your ego is so big you had to try and do it again. You got the same result. You are not going to piss on my parade. You treat me like shit at work and even said I am not worthy of wearing this jacket. Tonight you found out otherwise. You piss me off. I don't deserve this shit from you. I got this job because I worked my ass for it.

I earned it, just like I earned tonight. You're a cunt. Are we done now? Cheers!" I let him have it. I raised my beer bottle to him at 'cheers.' Whoever told me there was nothing more fragile than a man's ego was dead right. They have even to try to piss on another's parade to bring them down with them.

I went back over to my crew and finished celebrating. I even toasted the butt-hurt double victory. I think that was the best part. My team laughed and raised their glasses very eagerly to that toast.

I told them what was said. My team was shocked but not shocked. More shocked, Team Butt-Hurt had the guts to say it to my face. Any other time it is behind my back. Alcohol is a truth serum. I had a few too. I may have said more, but don't give a shit.

* * *

I went to work the next day with my medal and trophy in hand. I had to show the rest. The other former dishwashers needed to see we won. We won against Team Butt-Hurt twice. Chef Joyce looked over at me and smiled.

"We have another announcement this morning?" she asked

"We got People's Choice last night!" I shouted, holding up our trophy. Applause. Of course, a few sour looks from those who treated us like garbage.

The award still hangs up in the kitchen. I kept my medal. It brings a smile to my face when I look at it. I was also part of the winning team the next year as the co-captain. My medals hang proudly on my wall sconces in my dining room. I think of that jealous sore loser every time I look at them. Some will tear you down, but your accomplishments outshine their negativity.

I got an excellent Facebook post I shared. "Don't kill your haters with kindness. Torture them with success." Hell yeah. I love it.

Chapter 8

It was back to work as usual. We had people in this kitchen who did not know their elbow from their asshole. The lack of experience of the unwillingness to learn, unfortunately, happens a lot. It is a plague in every kitchen.

We had one guy who just stood around picking his nose and teeth—he was a downright disgusting pig. How many ties he got told to wash his hands. That idiot should not even be allowed near food ever. He even tried to say he was allergic to heat. The old saying comes into play. If you can't take the heat, get out of the kitchen. These idiots would run to their doctors to get notes to get out of doing the tasks they didn't want to do.

Simple solution. If you can't do the job, get the fuck out! If you can't do the job- get the fuck out! Nobody likes to carry dead weight.

This behaviour is definitely where my hatred of excuses comes from. The same people were getting away with the same shit every day. Anywhere else, their employment would be terminated.

A cook who can't be around heat. GET THE FUCK OUT! You are fucking lazy and useless! There is nothing worse than when this shit is allowed to continue when management should crush it immediately. In my kitchen today, it is immediately squashed. I weed them out quickly.

Check your local labour laws and act appropriately. Get rid of your problems as quickly as you can. If not, they will be much bigger and more challenging to get rid of later.

There was one person who worked in the dessert area. She never cut her pies with a knife but rather a pie lifter. I watched her cut a round cake straight across rather than in wedges. In some slices, you got globs of icing and not cake. Are you kidding me?! I have seen stupidity before, but this takes the cake.

I could remain silent no longer. I snatched a piece of 'cake' icing glob and showed the Chef. I was losing my mind. I couldn't believe this type of stupidity existed, plus the fact she had been doing this job for ten years! Unbelievable.

I was even more pissed at the fact the old Chef would not dishwashers cook but allowed morons like this to keep their jobs. I was professionally trained and had to work with complete idiots set in their ways for more than ten years.

Thankfully they listened and taught dumbass how to cut a cake. It's basic skills. Even at family gatherings, if it is round, it is cut in wedges. How do you eat a slice of pizza when it round? By the wedge, stupid.

If it is square or rectangle, cut into squares or bars. The basics, and yet you will have those who are stupefied by the obvious. I stayed in this place for eight years. If you think that is it, it is far from it. Stupidity can be rampant and usually is.

* * *

Let's stick to the dessert area for a while. How hard is it to make a crepe with ready-made crepe batter? Pretty easy, right. How sad would it be if I told you that some people couldn't even give a basic crepe batter?

Let me help you with that. The simple ingredients of crepes are flour, eggs, milk, water, salt and butter. Place the batter over medium heat and spread thinly until lightly golden brown. Flip and brown the other side.

You would think it is easy, right? Nope, We had some like Helen, who would put the batter about half an inch thick and make football-shaped doughy slop for guests. Their reasoning was because they could get more on the crepe iron without cluing into the fact that their half-inch thick footballs took longer to cook than the 2 minutes it takes to do the job correctly. Also, when you do it properly, it tastes better.

Their way is always better, and they know more because they have been doing incorrectly so long. One would use a 2 oz ladle to try and thin it rather than use a spatula. Watching her try and spread the batter with the 2 oz ladle on a crepe iron was painful to watch. It's like trying to serve someone serve the soup with a teaspoon from the pot to the bowl—a waste of time. Work smarter, not harder. I associated smarter with this twit. Smart is not in the wheelhouse here.

We had guests who would ask for well-done crepes. Remember what doneness applies to meat? Yup, a well-done crepe. So overcooked it was full of holes and broke apart when you tried to fold it. It's burnt. Now let's add that to Helen's footballs. Is it time-saving or time-wasting? Had they been made right, we would not have had guests always asking for well-done crepes—Thick, doughy and chewy.

* * *

I kept a good relationship with the dishwashers as you should. I am about respect and treating others the way you want. It is the Golden Rule. It's in every culture and religion. It goes a long way. Even when I am a Sous Chef, I always jump in to help the dishwashers. Every member of your team is essential.

Here are my thoughts; if you ever think you are too good to treat your staff with respect, you need to scrub a few pans. Everyone does dishes or helps stack. I find it keeps me grounded. You do dishes at home, so no matter how big your ego is, it isn't that big you can't wash a dish.

I like to joke with my dishwashers. They will ask me for something, and I respond, "That is not my job." They know I am kidding, and we laugh. Of course, I do it for them. And help out where I can.

These people have no respect for each other and not for the dishwashers either. They are disrespectful in every way. The first thing that comes out of their mouths is a complaint. "Why isn't this done?" "Where's that?" not a "Hello," bitch and complain and look for something to go snitch to the sous chef. It is worse than a high school. Heaven forbid you to have to do some work. A proper handoff is picking up where the other person left off. You don't come in and attack the other person. It shows you are a bitter no class piece of shit when you do.

* * *

Let's talk about pasta for a bit. It should be a simple thing to do—boil noodles al dente. Add sauce and serve. Making sauces is an art and takes time and must be done right. I got good at them and got taught how to make them by an Italian chef properly. She is amazing. I love a Bolognese or meat sauce. It's comfort food for me. She always gave me shit for not cooking them long enough. "Cook it!" "Make my Nona proud!" She drilled that into me well.

When cooking pasta, keep this in mind:

1. Water should be salty like the ocean.
2. Cook the pasta to Al Dente, which means to the tooth. Still firm when bitten. 8-9 minutes from a rolling boil.
3. Never rinse off the pasta. It rinses off the starch, and your sauce will not stick to it.
4. Put the pasta on a baking sheet with parchment to cool. Toss in olive or canola oil to prevent sticking or drying out. Reheat later in small batches for service. At home, drain the pasta and serve with your favourite sauce. Never rinse pasta. Never throw it at the wall. Were you raised in a barn? Taste it. Set your timer.

I suggest finding a recipe that works well for you. I like to mix beef and pork in mine, same as my meatballs. Due to some diets and beliefs, but the fat content makes a great sauce or meatball. You will get into a discussion for red or white wine or none at all. I prefer red wine with red meats, and the basic rule is never to cook with a wine you won't drink.

In professional kitchens, the cooking wine is usually heavily salted, and you will have to adjust the seasoning accordingly.

If you open a jar of sauce and add Italian seasoning and ground beef to it, please get the hell out of my kitchen. It shows no respect for the food or the culture it originated. Go open a can of Chef Boyardee instead and enjoy.

Brown your beef and pork blend with a bit of olive oil. I like 50/50 or 60/40—season with salt and pepper. I like to use SPG. Salt, pepper, and garlic at a ratio of 70% salt, 15% pepper and 15% garlic. Add onions and some fresh garlic, oregano, basil. Add crushed tomatoes and tomato paste. You want to add your wine generally at the halfway point in the cooking process. Again, this is debatable as to who you talk with on the subject.

One thing agreed upon is that you never add it at the end as you want the alcohol to cook off and blend the flavours in the simmering process. Stir occasionally and garnish with freshly chopped basil.

I have a few favourites in pasta sauces and will cove them. Carbonara is excellent and has a great history to it. I did a little poking around d online for it, and it started by coal workers who prepared it on their shovels over a fire. Its name refers to the ground black pepper in the dish to resemble the coal from the miners. It is also a marriage between bacon and egg rations between American and Italian soldiers during the second world war.

Heat your olive oil, add your bacon or pancetta and cook until crispy; add garlic. On a side note, garlic cooks quickly and releases its aroma. The aroma is your indicator its cooking is done. Temper your eggs, heavy cream and cheese and add to your pasta. Garnish with fresh basil and back pepper.

I made this sauce ahead, and when I caught a particular individual tossing it out so she could use bechamel and bacon bits in a pan and said it was a better way to do it, I lost my shit. Not only was she inexperienced, but she claimed to have Italian heritage and do something that painfully stupid. It was infuriating.

Bechamel is milk, butter and flour. Oh, but she added bacon bits. Yeah, that makes this so much better. Disgusting and downright disrespectful to her own culture. One of my biggest pet peeves is bastardizing a recipe to cut corners and disrespecting the culture from which it came. Would Nona stoop to that level? No way! That is just plain laziness and disrespect. I tasted like fucking shit and was devoid of flavour. No seasoning whatsoever. I would have terminated for turning out that shit. However, it was addressed. Your stupid is showing—Bechamel and bacon bits. I am still shaking my head on that one.

I like tomato sauce just for its simplicity. Sometimes it is the simple things in life that make things better. I can have a terrible day, and a nice bowl of pasta and tomato sauce with fresh basil and cheese can make it all better. I'm just saying. Try it, and a nice bottle of Sangiovese helps. It's my go-to pizza and pasta wine. Chianti is a region in Tuscany. A Chianti wine comes from that region. I love that too, even though it is the same grape. It's the region. It sounds fancy to say Chianti.

Marinara sauce traditionally contained seafood. Marinara means Mariners. It was what fishermen used to cook their fish. In America, there is no seafood in it, and it is a tomato sauce.

For singles who are learning to cook, this is a great date night dish. Make a nice salad, toasted garlic bread and cheese, maybe add some meatballs as an option. It is entirely up to you and always serve with a Sangiovese wine and some good quality cheese(s). Cannolis or tiramisu for dessert will help the night too.

Alfredo is a cream-based sauce, and it is acceptable to use Bechamel for this one. Adding fresh garlic, nutmeg, and parsley to your bechamel sauce will make a quick and easy Alfredo sauce. Had dumbass been doing this in a pan, I would have had no issues with it. It is a sample sauce and can be made a la minute in a pan due to its simplicity. The Bechamel and bacon bits are nothing short of blasphemy and are entirely shameful.

Another cook put full-size raw crudites of broccoli, cauliflower and baby carrots in Bechamel. It was left for me to make Primavera Sauce. It's a shake-your-head moment. I a[[reciate the gesture somewhat but don't mix them. Leave them as a mise en place.

Some Basic Kitchen Rules:

1. Taste your food.
2. Read your chits, and double-check them before sending them out.
3. If you wouldn't eat it- don't serve it. The chances are your guests won't either.
4. When in doubt, throw it out. (If you are unsure how old an item is or don't like the smell- toss it)
5. Label and date everything
6. Clean up as you go
7. Follow proper food handling
8. Be respectful.
9. Swearing is okay but not directed at another person. (My rule)
10. Avoid hateful homophobic and racial slurs. (This should be a given, but there is always one person. My other rule)
11. Your opinion is not in the recipe
12. Your urgency is not my emergency
13. The Chef is in charge, not you

Chapter 9

There are always different personalities in every workplace. We had them all. There was a group of lazy, useless fucks who used every excuse to get out of doing tasks they didn't want to do. My favourite was, "I never did that before." We had weak management who let this go on for years. When I say years, I mean years like a minimum of 10!

"Can you cover a break?"

"I never worked there before." The person gets excused; get someone else.

"Can you work this station?"

"I never did that before," They get excused.

I have had multiple situations where these people would assign themselves to simple areas like salad and dessert. Do the minimal and let everyone else do the hard work. Lazy and just taking up space. If this group were assigned elsewhere, they would deliberately fuck up or fall behind.

I was tournant (Jack of all trades) at this point and ad to do breaks and assist where needed. I lost my mind when we called Tess to make Chicken Fried Rice, white rice for the Asian area, and four stir-fries with premade sauces. Here's what she did in 3 hours of prep time: she got the vegetables out, put out the extra sauces like plum and sweet and sour, made white rice, failed to turn on the deep fryer(soggy wet spring rolls as a result), and a vegetable stir fry.

Her chicken fried rice was where I lost my mind. She heated the rice in the steamer and put it in the rice server. There was no chicken, seasoning, soy sauce, or vegetables whatsoever. Nope, too busy socializing at the dessert station or visiting her friend at the salad bar. Of course, they let it slide, and I get to fix it for her lazy ass. She should have been disciplined or, in my opinion-fired. That behaviour is entirely inexcusable. In my kitchen, her ass would have been gone. No exceptions.

CHICKEN FRIED RICE INGREDIENTS

Brown rice
Chicken breasts
Sesame oil
Vegetable oil
Green onions
Garlic
Eggs
Soy sauce
Saly and pepper to taste
Carrots and peas (frozen is preferred)

The chicken is precooked that we had. It takes like ten minutes at most do. The rice was hot, so frying it in a wok with the other ingredients and adding scrambled eggs should not be hard. Taste it as you go. I know it's hard. It is the same as turning on a dep fryer and letting it get to temperature. Teenagers at fast food joints do a better job than these grown-ass adults. They know standards because they are correctly taught from the start. These adults are sad and pathetic.

There was another dumb ass that occasionally worked the area. Dan liked to put cucumbers in his stir-fries. Yes, you read that right.

Cucumbers in stir fry. I have yet to eat any Asian restaurant that puts fucking cucumbers in their stir fry. Creativity should be squashed when there is no fundamental understanding of how things work or what goes together to make a dish. Standard recipes are there for a reason; this would be one of them.

Now that I mentioned a standard recipe. A standard recipe is used to control cost and quantity. It contains the ingredients and method of preparing it. There are the reasons we use these in the industry. They are:

1. The recipe is tried, tested and true.
2. Portion control
3. Reduces errors
4. Consistency in taste, portion, quality. For this, I will use a famous fast-food burger. That burger tastes the same and is the same size no matter where you go from coast to coast. Consistency is what a guest expects every time they visit.

Dan got to make sushi one day. You know it was an abomination. He used leftover roast beef to make it. It was served. It ultimately made my day when the executive sous chef was walking by and saw it. He did a double-take and stopped.

"What the fuck is this?" he asked.

"Roast beef sushi, Chef. Dan's specialty. It tastes like ass, but they want it out anyway. Guests have been complaining," I stated.

He took one and took a bite. The look of disgust went across his face in mid-chew. He came around the entrance of the station and spat it in the garbage.

"Get rid of it. Jesus Christ, we are raising the bar here, aren't we?" he asked sarcastically. I could hardly hide my delight. It was about time someone saw the fuckery I saw daily. Letting the intellectually challenged near food and encouraging creativity is not a good combination.

"With pleasure," I replied and dumped that shit in the trash where it belonged.

* * *

Chefs are funny people too. We are sarcastic, crass and crude at times. I will give you another chance to laugh at me. I had about 5 gallons of gravy in a Cambro to go in the hotel pans for the reheated roast beef I would do. Another cook came into the kitchen and bumped the table, and I tried to save it from falling on the floor. Nope.

The whole 5 gallons slid off the table and landed right side up. It shot a wave of cold brown gravy and covered me from head to toe. I had to wipe it out of my eyes even to see. When I have the others, come running in after hearing, "Hey, get in here and look at this!"

Thanks, Chris. I had an audience on this one, and they were laughing hysterically at my ass. It is not the first time I had to shower and change at work. I will cover those in a minute. When you leave the kitchen covered head to toe in gravy, you will get laughter, pointing, and questions.

"Oh my God, what happened?" asked another employee

"I'm fucking marinading," I shot back. I was not in the mood for stupid questions. Another person asked the same question. "I'm starting a new fucking fashion trend," I answered. Then again, I get asked on my way to the showers. "I stood behind someone who had Mexican food." The look on that person's face was priceless. I am covered in brown gravy.

I had a shower and changed my clothes. A co-worker and friend went to get me a new uniform from the uniform locker. He couldn't stop laughing. Dishwashing was not too happy with me for the mess it made, but they found it funny at the same time. I worked with them all, and they knew my demeanour which probably made it more hilarious.

Yes, I swear and cuss. I make inappropriate jokes. It happens all the time in the kitchen, just like when I worked in factories. Profanity is the norm. However, in my kitchen, I do not allow it to be used against another person. It becomes a hostile environment and personal attacks. In self-defence, have at it. Let the abuser have it.

I have done it. Suppose you can make the abuser cry? Even better. I will buy you a drink. That is how I got my nickname Peachka. It is

Hungarian for cunt. It sounds nicer in other languages. In Italian, it is Frenya. It sounds like a spice.

Now a few more laughs. When you work in a large property, you will have all kinds of staff with all sorts of personalities. I learned the hard way to make sure you flush the toilet before sitting on it. We had a staff member who liked to flush diapers.

Yup, there is nothing like taking a shit, and when you go to do a courtesy flush, the whole thing backs up all over your clothes and floods the restroom. Your log and all. Water everywhere and going out the door into the hallway. When you sit, you are committed to the prank. It is not funny.

It is disgusting. It ruined my phone, and I had to send another employee to the kitchen to get one of my friends once again. They were howling with laughter. Yup, being covered in my shit is hilarious. It's a fucking scream. Okay, I will be honest. It is funny if it happens to someone else. Not me. You would think the same. I am just glad it happened before Tik Tok became a thing. I could only think of what music that video would have been compiled. The Pepto Bismal song? Upset stomach, nausea, heartburn and diarrhea? I am sure a search engine search would have a list.

Chapter 10

One thing I can't stand is baby talk. It just makes my blood boil. I find it repulsive. I would not be surprised if babies find it stupid too. I can't stand it. My mother dated a guy who used it, and it made my stomach turn. Suppose I could roll me yes any louder? It is not cute at all. When an adult does it regularly to try and get her way, I find it desperate and obvious. I want to punch you right in the throat.

I had her on my line a few times. She would take extra breaks and whine and cry about anything. She is a mousy, baby-talking, talentless, whiny little bitch. If she didn't get her way, she would play sick and go home. I despised her. Her name was Tracy.

I had the Italian area, and I set it up. Tracy came in at 11 and didn't want to make pasta. She only wanted to make pizza on the premade dough. She cried when she had to make pasta. Are you kidding me? I refused to let her do anything else. I don't give in to sucking and whining or excuses. So your damn job. You were hired to do a job. Do it. You make the same wage as everyone else to do the same amount of work as everyone else. So again, please do it. If you can't do the job- get the fuck out. Your ass can be replaced in 5 minutes.

"When you don't let me do what I want, it makes me feel bad," She whined.

"I don't give a shit. You take extra breaks and do next to no work. You whine and cry to get your way. That shit doesn't work with me. Get your ass over there. I am sick of your baby talking and your bullshit," I replied.

"But I want pizza."

"I don't give a fuck what you want. Earn your wage like everyone else. You cry about working the salad bar. You only want to do desserts and pizza. You are a useless, lazy, whiney, mousy little bitch. Your baby talk is annoying. Shut the fuck up and do your job. I don't want to hear you baby talk. It's nauseating, and it's insulting when you do it to an adult." I shot back at her.

"You're making me feel bad," the little bitch started to put the waterworks on.

"Oh wah! Oh, you are making me feel bad," I mocked her right to her face. I do that to people when I have no respect for them: a snitch, a lazy piece of shit, and a shit disturber. This bitch is all three. She left crying to the Chef.

I got pulled into his office, and we had to have a chat about others' feelings. I am seriously going to vomit. People can whine and cry and make excuses why they can't do their job. Now I have to care about their precious little feelings? Bullshit.

"I sent her home because she was crying. She said you were mean to her.," he started.

"I am going to cut you off right there. You know we have a group that whines and cries to get out of work. 'I never did that before,' and they have you conditioned to letting them get away with it. You guys, as in management, have enabled this for years. I m not. She comes over to where I am, she is working, and it will not be what she wants. She gets paid the same as everyone else, and it's time they got off their ass and learned. They make me sick," I replied

"Not everyone has the same skill level," he replied.

"No. I am not accepting that excuse. That little bitch has been in this department for 15 years. How long are these excuses going to continue before you clue in and realize they are dead weight? There is an excuse for everything. Suppose you can't do the job-leave. I am not enabling her ever, and we can have all the chats you want. It is not changing. I am sick and tired of it just like the rest of the crew Whining and crying to get their way, and the stupid lazy get coddled when they should be out on their ass."

"I need you to be more empathetic," he continued. I pulled out my phone.

"The average person works 2,000 hours a year. That is 250 days per year. Lazy bitch has been pulling this shit for 15 years. That is more than 3,750 days of excuses. So, Nope. Not happening; she had 15 years to learn. I'm not here to wipe her ass for her and am not starting now. She can cry all she wants and go on stress leave for all I care. Her contributions are so minuscule nobody will notice she's gone. That's how much work she does. The only thing she needs is a good swift kick in the fucking ass. Can I go now?" I have not patience for the feelings of the weak and lazy. I still don't. Pull the line or hit the road.

"Go ahead," he replied. Just as a side note, the mousy bitch was on leave for three months. Pathetic. However, it was a blessing not having her around. Too bad it wasn't permanent.

* * *

It's Insult time. In the kitchen, you will hear several. Mousy bitch is so clueless that it would be the fastest trip in America if she had an idea go through her head.

* * *

One of my coworkers had to put one guy in his place. He thought he was all that. You're so pathetic that your perfect date is a jar of peanut butter at the petting zoo.

* * *

One of my originals: Your food is so disgusting it should be served at the emergency room in place of ipecac. If you are not sure what it is, it is to induce vomiting for poisoning. I have seen some that would cause vomiting by looking at it. Fucking disgusting

* * *

Another one: Your food is so disgusting it should be on a Weight Watchers pamphlet to ensure a loss of appetite.

* * *

I saw one plate online that looked like someone took a shit on the plate. It was a blood sausage, but it did not look appealing at all. I had the perfect C-shaped curve to it as well. The only thing that piece of shit was missing was pieces of corn in it. The side dishes served with it looked like gelatinous blobs splattered on the plate. The beans looked dry and overcooked to the point where the structural integrity has broken down. The macaroni and cheese had overcooked pasta that was mush and held together by a dried-out cheese sauce. Play-doh looks more appetizing.

The 'Chef' that posted this online was proud of it and wanted feedback. She got it. Not one positive comment, and then she got butt-hurt because of it. Put that on a menu and see what happens. No customer would accept it. It is not appetizing. It is repulsive. We eat with our eyes, and my eyes were saying, 'Hell no.'

* * *

I love the roast my dish things on social media. Some will put up some of the most disgusting things to get humorous comments from other chefs. One put up a chicken breast with a yellow-greenish pesto sauce that looked like something out of a Sexually Transmitted Disease information pamphlet. I called it Chicken Ghonorrea. We are horrible, but it is in good fun.

* * *

The worst insult I ever saw on a chef page was a pasta dish loaded with cheese and a lumpy tomato sauce. It looked like something out of a horror movie or a lab experiment has gone horrifically wrong. One chef summed it up as abortion waste. Crude but fitting.

* * *

Every chef knows the rod to clean the fryer and unclog the drainage hole for the debris that falls into the cold zone of the fryer is the abortion tool. I don't know the origin, but it is a commonplace term.

* * *

One that never gets old is tossing a salad. It's slang for a rim job. Licking your asshole. It's always funny when a co-worker asks you to toss the salad or offer it with a bowl of mixed greens. When using this one, make sure you have a salad in a bowl if you have a snowflake nearby.

* * *

I had a cook I worked with ask me if I would like to suck him off. He was overweight, so I went right for the kill.

"Yeah. You're a dream come true—everything I ever wanted. I want to lift 100 pounds of fat to get to something as small as a thimble.

I am quick-witted and was trained well by my late aunt. She and I shared sarcasm. She taught me I could insult someone to their face, and they will laugh. I do it all of the time. Do it with a smile, and the dumb shits think you are joking. It's lots of fun. I have mastered it.

I wore a t-shirt to work with Smartass University on it. It's hilarious when your old department manager sees you in the hallway with it.

"Nice shirt. You're the Dean," he commented.

"Yup, I should be," I replied.

You can add the fact I have zero fucks to give. Your wimpy ass feelings don't mean shit to me. If you are an asshole, I will call it out. If your food tastes like shit, I will tell you. I am not here to wipe your ass for you in the kitchen, nor am I here to talk about your feelings. If you want to talk about feelings, there are counselling numbers for that, and you can bore the shit out of them, not me.

If you have a legitimate problem, I can steer you in the right direction. If you need assistance, there are places to call. I am not a therapist.

My favourite sign I ever saw was "President of the DILLIGAFF Club.

DILLIGAFF is an acronym for Do I Look Like I Give A Flying Fuck. Very suiting.

The Dean of Smartass University and the President of the DILLIGAFF Club.

Chapter 11

Snitches always come in the workplace. There are lots of articles out there to weed them out. As a leader, you should know they lie to deflect attention from themselves and their constant underperformance. It works the same way with children when they are looking for favouritism or a treat. Usually, they are guilty of something else, and it is always a deflection and manipulation to take the heat off of them and put it on someone else instead. So in the lazy little bitch's case, it was because she took excessive breaks, did minimal work, whines, and even puts on the waterworks as a deflection ploy to deflect the attention off of her and her substandard performance.

Females are great at putting on the waterworks to try and get out of trouble, and they are rightfully disciplined. It is a learned trait from childhood. They are putting on the waterworks to manipulate your parents. They cause shit, and when they get caught, here comes the waterworks. It is a deflection ploy and usually tries to assign the blame to someone else. Allowing and entertaining this behaviour enables it to continue well into adulthood. You create a snitch and a manipulative little bitch.

Males who develop this behaviour are great at lying and passing the blame on others. Again, it all starts as a kid. Go and cause problems and then go running to their parents and play the victim. You can bet they are the same persons who like to start their bullshit on social media and report you to moderators when you tell them off. Females do it too. They have learned how to get away with it. It's funny how these were also members of the "I Never Did That Before" crew. Do you see the pattern? It's nothing a good old-fashioned ass-whooping couldn't cure.

I had a few instances when I dealt with snitches where they admitted to their shit disturbing and then put on the waterworks to try and get out of it. Hell no. They got what they had coming. Never back down. Give them what they deserve. In the workplace, it is discipline and suspensions up to and including termination. Document, document and document and then nail their ass. Quit your fucking snitching and shit disturbing or join the unemployment line. If you are a manager that entertains and engages in this behaviour, I hope you like hiring and training. Nobody will stay and put up with your shit. I will cover this later.

Snitches are poison to your work environment and can't be trusted whatsoever. They like to run their mouths about co-workers, so imagine what they say about you in management. The reality is that a snitch has nothing good to say about anyone and will always run behind anyone's back to talk shit and try to make themselves look good. They are miserable and are not happy unless everyone else is just as miserable too. Seek professional help if you are unhappy. You suck at your job and need to mind your own business.

You have to have trust in any work environment to keep it harmonious. Once you have one of these parasites, it will kill morale and cause a decrease in productivity. Do you want to be friends with a lying, backstabbing piece of shit? I didn't think so.

Snitches are usually liars too. They love to embellish and make up all kinds of shit. You will never get the whole truth from them either. You will get only the parts that benefit them if you get any truth at all. Their faults are always passed off to someone else in a desperate ploy to try and make themselves look better. So I will change the statement from "snitched are usually liars" to "Snitches are lying fucks."

There is a difference between a snitch and a whistle-blower. The critical difference is when it comes to unethical, dangerous behaviour that puts others at risk or in danger. Everyone is responsible for reporting severe conduct violations such as sexual harassment, violence, including to themselves, and theft. For example, if someone is talking bout murder or suicide- report it immediately. Protecting the safety and well-being of others is not snitching.

Snitches look for trivial things like an extra 5 minutes of breaks a co-worker took, a smoke break, missing proper shoes, such as wearing white shoes when black is required, an employee is a few minutes late for work and so on. I will touch on a snitch I had dealings with whom we nicknamed Fat Rat Ass Bitch. All good things come to those who wait. First, we will go over the traits of a snitch so you can spot them and take the appropriate actions.

How to spot one and flush them out is pretty simple. A snitch is usually the weakest link. A snitch usually has poor performance, gets denied any advancement, or is jealous of their co-workers' accomplishments and resorts to snitching to try and drag everyone else down with them. They try to make themselves look more favourable to management by trashing others. A snitch is mad at the world, and as long as someone pays for it, who cares? Nobody likes a complainer, so squealing is the alternative, but it rarely pays off. It is childish high school behaviour, and they were probably a loser there too.

Disrespectful behaviour is based on jealousy. If the person trashes others in public, there is a pretty good chance that they are your snitch. As a manager, if you think they only belittle their peers, you are naïve. You can bet they trash talk you too. I will be willing to put money on it, especially if you don't reward them for being a "model employee."

Watch out for someone in general or common areas sitting by themselves. They are eavesdropping in on all the gossip and pick up on any negative detail on their peers. I had seen some taking notes when they had their little pad concealed in a crossword puzzle book. If that person always seems to be there, is it a coincidence? Probably not.

This next trait is revolting. Ass kissing and snitching go hand in hand. A snitch is also a kiss ass and sucks up to management. It is nauseating how they try and suck up. A snitch loves to point out anything they see to be wrong on your part to try and make themselves look good and how well they follow company policies and procedures. They are always trying to make themselves look better to the boss. The brown noser is more than likely your snitch. They are always looking for praise.

A snitch loves to work long hours and does minimal work because they take mental notes of everyone else's movements. Don't be surprised if they have an actual notebook. I have seen one as a union rep more times than I care to count. This behaviour is to be squashed by the union or management. If you feel you are being watched, you probably are. Also, if they meet any of the other signs mentioned, you pretty much found your snitch.

The best defence is keeping your mouth shut. Keep it professional, and don't give out too much personal information. Stick to work-related items and watch out. A snitch likes to lie and manipulate any detail they can. They are desperate for recognition and some form of reward. I blame the participation ribbon for this as well. Not everyone can be a winner. Doing a shit job in school got you a participation ribbon or part marks. The real world does not work that way. Sorry. There are winners, and there are losers. If you are a snitch- you're a loser and a sore one at that.

Keep your head down and do a good job. A well-done job always thwarts a snitch; however, they will be all over it if you make a significant mistake. They like to sabotage you as well. If you feel you are being set up, you are. Snitches love to try that stunt and hope they can swoop in and save the day to try and make themselves look better. Never stop to a snitch's level. You only hurt yourself. They have no problem trying to take credit for someone else's work. I will cover this in a bit. Team Butt-hurt.

Reacting out of anger gives the snitch power that their lies may be true because you are defensive. These people are cunning and manipulative liars. The favourite game is cause shit and plays the victim when you call them out or lash out at them. You are mean and what they said is true, right? Did you have a sibling pull this behaviour when you were growing up? I will bet you did. These fuckers are good at the game now.

Do not leave anything personal around. If you work in an office, never use personal email and clear your browser history. A snitch has no problem going through your private space looking for juicy details. Desperate times call for desperate measures, right?

When I have a kiss ass and a snitch on the management level, I know what they are up to something. If you give them any reward, it encourages the behaviour. Think of Pavlov when you are giving out any type of reward. Pavlov did lots of experiments on this subject. It is a good read. The snitch will connect the prize to a job well done, and you can bet it will escalate as they need that attention and reward. The more you entertain and reward, the more they do it. You are enabling and encouraging this behaviour. Fostering this is a sign of a weak and poor manager.

Snitching must be nipped in the ass immediately. It creates a hostile and poisoned environment. There have to be consequences to a snitch. I like to get rid of snitches through progressive discipline. I had a manager who rewarded it and even disciplined other employees based on snitches reports even though they were lies, but her little kiss ass could never do such a thing. I will cover this later. I promise.

Pile the work on them and keep them busy no matter how trivial the tasks are. I recommend unfavourable jobs like heavy cleaning and the nastier, the better. Grease traps are great for this and other neglected areas like behind the dishwasher in the kitchen. In an office, there is always a job that everyone hates. It's perfect for snitches—the more mundane, the better.

I also like to isolate that snitch. Make them work alone with tedious, meaningless work—the more time-consuming, the better. Sorting silverware and polishing it can be fun. Peeling potatoes is another fun one or just dicing onions by hand. Keep them at room temperature since they like putting on the waterworks. Please make sure they are nice and robust Spanish onions. Let the tears flow.

If any of the strategies fail- fire their ass. Document everything when it comes to snitches. Snitches destroy productivity and morale. You suck as a manager when you entertain a snitch. You are just as guilty for killing the environment by engaging a lying fucking snitch.

I always love it when these people fall on hard times and nobody is there to help. I worked with a snitch we nicknamed Fat Rat Ass Bitch. When she got cancer, her only two friends tried to get a collection for her. Most of us laughed in their face and had no problem telling them we hope she suffers and dies. May the urine flow freely on your grave bitch. Do you want to be this hated? Shut the fuck up and mind your own business. I also love the joke-what is red and bad for your teeth? A brick- shut the fuck up and mind your own business.

There is a saying that snitches belong in ditches or snitches get stitches. Heed the warning. You are a dangerous road when your co-workers would love to kick you in the face and stomp on your throat. Curb stomping is a good option as well. That is about as much respect as a lying snitch deserves—throat punch Thursdays. I am facetious. Violence is never the answer. This trash is not worth the jail time. They are desperate losers. The worse part is if you are a snitch and your co-workers could get away with disposing of you, they would.

Destroying their credibility and any chance for reward is the best way to handle them. Exposing them for what they are works too. Document and follow your chain of command. Have witnesses. Make sure you walk straight and narrow when you do. It can take a while to get rid of them. Be very careful as they may have friends in management, and you will have a weak manager who happens to be their ally. I have had this happen. It is coming later. The manager was tight with this group. The place was full of snitches.

Chapter 12

I brought her up, and now it's time to discuss Fat Rat Ass Bitch. I am not going to use her real name, so I searched for female pig names. I was going to call her Petunia. It's also a flower, and she is a blooming idiot. Then I searched the Urban Dictionary. Buela wins. The definition is someone who is extremely ugly. This swine is ugly inside and out like any other piece-of-shit snitch. How fitting.

Buela is about 350 pounds of a fat self-loathing, lying, manipulative, conniving, hypocrite bitch. She claims to be a Christian and uses that as a deflection shield for her shit too. I will bet even Jesus thinks she is a piece of shit. That is another one that makes me laugh. Try and bring your belief in a deity into it and think you are above reproach. You are hiding behind your faith as another deflection ploy. Trying to put yourself above your lying bullshit because you have an imaginary friend doesn't cut it. Even Jesus thinks you are a piece of shit. Pathetic. Guess what? The rest of us see through it. As soon as you do that, we know your ass is lying.

Buela never advanced past a prep cook and loved to snitch on anyone she can. She is fat and lazy. One of her little games was walking around and looking at what everyone else has done and going through their stations and fridges, looking for anything she felt was out of place. She would never lift a finger to help anyone when they were in the weeds and getting jacked. She liked to watch them struggle. It would be a shame if she ever broke a sweat other than waddling her fat ass around the kitchen looking for someone to snitch on.

She liked playing the victim and crying just like the mousy little bitch when she got called out. The truth always hurt her feelings. Snitching is a form of bullying. You are trying to get others in shit because you can't lift your shelbows high enough to hit them, and you are weak and will lose in a physical altercation. Having to resort to childish antics is pretty much the bottom of the barrel. As an adult, it is shameful, and your pathetic lost little loser shines through.

Didn't you have friends growing up? It's hard to imagine why not. You were probably the same jealous loser who didn't apply yourself in anything, and it was always somebody else's fault. You sucked at sports because they wouldn't let you play. No. It was because you were too busy stuffing yourself with junk food and didn't want to play. Running some of the fat off of your ass would have done you some good. You probably hated the athletic girls because the boys found them attractive. Girls found them attractive too.

Buela also liked to take pictures of other people's areas with her phone and run to the office to squeal like the fucking pig she is. Suuuueeeeyyyyyy! There was not a single person in the kitchen she didn't snitch on. She took pictures of the break sheet. She always took extra breaks too. Typical hypocrite- do as I say, not as I do.

Mousy bitch liked to go on break at 11:30 and put 11:45 as her sign-out time and take half an hour instead of 15 minutes. When I was the breaker, I let that be known. Breaks were timed for 15 minutes as a breaker, and I only gave you 15 minutes. If you were not back, I let your area fall apart after the 15 minutes were up.

I love the Golden Rule of "Doing unto others" Some should be thankful, and lying trash like this should be afraid. The dumb ass thought I would cover her. She can lie and snitch and was stupid enough to think I would cover for her. Nope. Not a chance in Hell. I sunk them both. When asked, I pointed out their little game—the joy of killing two birds with one stone. Be careful who you try and fuck. If you are going to fuck me, you better have a bigger dick than I do.

Buela was also known for manipulating doctor's notes to suit her needs, just like Moussy Bitch. She had a doctor's note where she couldn't lift and tried to get others to do it for her. I outright refused to help her. I know a fucking liar when I see one. A lot of the time, doctors will write what you ask them. Snitches know this and will do anything to try and gain pity and win people over to their side. A case in point was the other loser who got his doctor to write he could not be around heat in a kitchen—shameful behaviour.

A pity party is a desperate measure to try and manipulate others into doing things for you. If you want friends, be friendly. An excellent place to start is to stop your fucking lying and abusing others as well as being a snitch. Buela is the same fat bitch that got cancer and wondered why nobody would donate a dime to help her. She got management to suspend employees because of her lying shit.

That is a weak manager too. When they entertain snitches and call it reporting, it is when management has fallen for the ploy, and the snitch is very powerful now. Your workplace is ultra toxic now. Watch your staff quit when they get sick of your shit. We will cover that later on. I have a good one for that to use as an example. I have several. Yeah, Fat Rat Ass Bitch makes me want to contribute to help her. The only thing I would be glad to do is to help her commit suicide.

She has gone even to the point of relabelling the plastic wrap on prep like chopped vegetables and stocking her area with it with her writing. Remove the plastic wrap and put new plastic wrap on it with her writing and take it for herself in her area. Then she would run over, take a picture of the newly emptied space and try and throw the other person under the bus for not doing their job. Imagine that, a thief and a liar too.

It's tough to imagine why nobody would want to help her out in any way. She is a super lovely person and deserves our respect. Yeah, right. There are cameras in the building, and she was caught on camera with the theft of goods and relabelling stunt. Oops. Snitches usually hang themselves. Losers are good at one thing-Losing. That's what losers do.

Buela is probably an emotional eater. She eats because she is upset and nobody likes her. Then turn that self-loathing into a weapon against others because he is a fat, miserable, lying piece of shit. Someone has to pay for it. Nobody is to blame but you, bitch. It brought such joy to my heart when I found out she finally got fired for her shit. Good riddance. All snitches should end up at the curb. I have taken pleasure in firing a few myself.

If you are an owner and manager, pay attention to who is telling you what. Make notes. If a specific individual is always running to you and kissing your ass, ask yourself why. Knowing what you know now, you have a poisonous individual and respond appropriately. Toss that trash out as fast as you can.

Chapter 13

I have to add a few more laughs, but you will have to shake your head at the same time. The same idiot that couldn't make fried rice sent a customer to the Asian area to het up a piece of the pie in the steamer. Brilliant idea; let's make a hot and soggy mess. I caught her using the steamer for that purpose. The light does not go all the way on upstairs in this one. She is also the same oblivious dullard that went to light the Crème Brulee torch off of the wok and walked across the buffet with it lit. Unbelievably stupid and reckless.

I had a male coworker whose fucks up was allowed to continue until it became a real issue. He conditioned guests into thinking the carvery was a steakhouse. It started with a few where he grabbed the Montreal Steak Spice, put it on the prime rib, and slapped it on the charbroiler. Pure intellect at work. A high-fat piece of meat on a high-heat cooking appliance. What could go wrong?

You guessed it. We had flames twelve inches high and burnt prime rib. With the burnt prime rib, you get complaints. "It's burnt." Well, no shit Sherlock. Then his solution was to cut it thicker because that will help. Right? Yeah, now we have a thicker piece of meat that still bursts into flames due to the high-fat content, and now, because it is thicker, you get complaints it's tough.

When you work the carvery, it is essential to know how to slice meat. The thicker the slice in beef, the tougher it becomes. Remember at the beginning of the book where we went over the levels of doneness? Well-done beef is tough and can be like leather. With the added element of a thick slice, you can guarantee it will be tough when cooked well-done. You just doubled down on tough. You also just guaranteed an unenjoyable dining experience. Chewing on an old boot even with a fantastic cut of meat like prime rib, one of the most tender cuts you can get.

We are going back to the more you cook it, the tougher it gets. For the best results, Prime rib should not be cooked more than medium-rare with an internal temperature of 130-135 F. I suggest pulling it at rare as it will have carry-over cooking. So, it is best to remove it at 120-125 F.

HOW TO CUT BEEF

1. Look for the grain and its direction.
2. Use a sharp carving knife
3. Secure the beef with the carving fork
4. Trim off excess fat. Be sure to leave a little.
5. Slice thin ¼ inch slices against the grain. For example, if the fibres run left to the right, slice up and down. It breaks down the fibres and loosens them for tenderness.

Nowhere does it say to run a steak house t the carvery. It should pretty much show the lack of intelligence there—the prime rib steak house. The idea of the charbroiler is to give it a little touch up to the proper doneness, which should be no more than a few seconds not to let some idiot think he was they are a master Chef in a steak house. I can bet you understand why Chefs swear now. The stupidity is intense from many sides.

You would get guests who are in a hurry but want chicken breasts that take longer to cook, and they think they are funny and then have the audacity to complain that it takes too long even if you explained it takes the longest to cook.

I have been condescended to in that snotty, condescending tone that I hate, and I have no problem giving it back. I had one asshole come up to the grill for an omelette. Here's how the conversation went:

"Hey, I want three cheese omelettes. You know-1,2,3," said the asshole in that condescending tone I hate.

"Oh, you can count. Did you want a gold star with that?" I shot back in the same tone. There were a few other guests nearby, and they started laughing at him. I got applause.

"You deserve that one, asshole," said one lady to the asshole.

"How can I help you?" I asked the lady.

"A western, please," she replied.

"No problem," I replied and put hers n right away. Assholes can wait.

"Hey, how come you didn't put mine on?" asked the asshole.

"Oh, I'm sorry. I still am stuck at counting to one. It's going to take some before I can count to three. I am a slow learner. It may take a bit to get there." I replied n a condescending tone. I smiled at him. The lady was howling with laughter along with the other guests in line. You reap what you sow. If you want to be a fucking dick, I will be one too. I will do it with a smile.

It's like I said before; we are not here to take your abuse. You want to be rude and a condescending jerk; your order goes to the bottom of the pile. I did that when I delivered pizza as a teenager. Rude and not tip-you can wait, and your can bet your ass you did. Nobody gets paid enough to take abuse at work. You don't like that shit, don't do it to someone else. I had someone scream at me and call me a 'stupid little faggot' over a nickel before. I took one out of my pocket and threw it in their face.

When you get it back, you get what you deserve. You don't have the right to complain when you get it back, either. As far as I am concerned, you showed that behaviour is acceptable to you.

I served another five people before returning to Asshole's order because I wanted him to wait some more. He was getting heated, and

I didn't care. Don't be rude. I looked over and smiled. He scowled at me—tough shit.

"May I please have my omelettes now? I'm sorry," he pleaded

"Thank you. Of course, you can," I said, smiling at him. I made them very quickly and gave them to him.

"Thank you," he said politely.

"You're welcome," I said, smiling at him. Surprisingly he didn't complain. The next time he came in, he was pleasant for some reason.

People like to pull all kinds of shit when they go out to eat. A customer complained that he was allergic to Farfalle (Bowtie pasta), but he could have penne. Yup, allergic to a shape. I refused to make it. Pasta is pasta. A lot of their alleged food allergies are fabricated.

It is incredible how many people fell for the Gluten-Free craze because they thought they would lose weight. I watched one lady looking t all of the items in the buffet.

"Is this gluten-free? Is this gluten-free?" she asked, pointing to the mashed potatoes and vegetables. Fad diets are bullshit. Everyone wants a quick fix. The only thing about those is how you can be fleeced of cash to buy books, over-priced food in the false premise of losing weight without exercise.

"Do you even know what gluten is?" I asked.

"No, but I heard it was bad for you and makes you fat," she replied.

"Oh my god. Stop believing everything you see on the internet. It is false. Gluten is a protein found naturally in grains like wheat and rye," I replied.

"Ok, that's nice. Now is this gluten-free?" she asked, pointing to the mashed potatoes.

"Absolutely. It would be best if you loaded up on those. It's natural and should help you," I replied. I watched her load half of her plate with mashed potatoes, and then I pointed out some other high-calorie gluten-free items—a complete dullard who would not listen to anything. So be it. Load up on the calories, but all is good as long as it is gluten-free. I then watched her scarfing down pie for dessert. Pie crust has gluten, dumbass. I don't feel guilty. The misinformed will not listen to anything other than the misinformation they obtained on the internet, no matter how fucked up it is.

One young man thought gluten was a toxin. He was convinced it was slowly killing him, and somehow the government was involved. I could not even waste my time. The internet is so full of shit at times. You need not look further than the conspiracy theories during any crisis we have faced from Y2K to the Mayan Callender and beyond. There is a giant steaming pile of bullshit on the internet. You don't need a mouse; you need a shovel.

Fad diets are like shooting stars. It burns bright and quick, and then it's gone. These diets make false claims about rapid weight loss or how to improve your health through detox. You can name off several on your own. A quick search on fad diets, and you will find several.

According to research, 95% of diets fail. Fad diets all have similar traits. They leave you hungry, not sustainable for life, and they get you nowhere. They offer a rapid loss and have nothing to back it up. Every time I see a new one, I roll my eyes even louder. They are all bullshit. They misinform people into believing in a magic cure to their weight problem and fleece you of cash in the process. The use of ripped models is a sales pitch and a window display—basic marketing techniques. Beautiful people are selling whatever they are paid to sell.

Let's look at beer drinkers. Are they all lean and muscular men who drink it regularly? Nope. Are lean, young girls scarfing down potato chips daily? Nope. Advertising. If you put more significantly obese and less attractive persons on those high-calorie food ads, would you buy them? Probably not. Ad a large-breasted and lean girl and a young man with ripped abs, you will. It's sex appeal. Sex appeal is used to sell those fad diets that don't work. It shows what you want. Who doesn't wish to have ripped abs?

Make healthier choices and exercise; that is the best way to maintain a healthier lifestyle. Slow and steady wins the race. As food professionals, we see these bullshit diets come and go. We get constant questions from the misinformed, and sometimes you have to let them eat cake and potatoes, especially when they don't listen.

It always goes back to the Dunning-Kruger effect. They always think they are more intelligent and more gifted and more vital than they are.

Have you ever heard," Do you know who I am?"

I always reply," No. Am I supposed to?"

As for the person who thinks they know everything, a report I read said to ask them when the last time they changed their opinion was. If they can't admit it, they are not as bright as they appear.

Dealing with that, we had a Chef who would always respond "excellent." Behind his back, it was "excrement." I find it quite useful in some situations like you previously read.

"Excrement." It sums up the shit quite well.

Chapter 14

There are some things you should never do while working in a restaurant. Hugging your guests is probably not appropriate. Some would disagree; however, it can be invasive and unwelcomed. I avoid this as much as possible. A simple handshake is just fine, depending on the customs, of course. Keep a level of professionalism.

One that bothers me is when the server sits at my table. I find this unwelcomed, and you are not part of our group. Would you please go away? Some guests find it acceptable but probably not the best decision as you cross the line of professionalism.

Keep your personal life out of it. They are there to dine and have a good time, not to hear about your personal life. If they ask, keep it positive and happy and short fewer details, the better. Your kids are great, life is good, move on. Your guests are not your therapists.

It annoys me to see staff sitting at guest tables and hugging as well. It takes one complaint, and then action has to be taken. Schmoozing is another thing that crosses the line, especially when trying to manipulate a tip out of the guest. Give them excellent service and smile, don't schmooze. You will earn your tip appropriately.

For me, a huge one is when staff consume alcohol on the property after their shift is done and make a complete ass out of themselves. I had to cut off my kitchen manager when she became intoxicated to the point of being an obnoxious and noisy pain in the ass. There is nothing worse than when guests know the person is an employee and behaving in such a way. I just took the job as General Manager in this place where she was friendly with the owner. A very slippery slope.

Excessively loud giggling, inappropriate sexual comments about male patrons who could hear every word she said.

"I'll bet he has a huge dick," she shouted to her friend less than two feet away. Yes, the customer heard it.

"I'd love to suck that big cock!" she shouted, and yes, he heard that too. It's fucking embarrassing.

"Hey, baby. Are you looking for a good time? Woo Whoo!" she shouted some more.

We did everything we could to get her drunken ass into a cab and get her out of there between the bartender and me. She expected me to overrule the bartender and keep serving her.

She later turned out to be a lying snitch because how dare cut her off alcohol service. The lies she made up were outlandish. It didn't help when the owner's role model kitchen manager was sucking off one of the cooks in the parking lot in her car while they were both on the clock. Sucking cock on the clock. She finished blowing him just before his wife came to pick him up. I know she swallowed every drop. She bragged about it as well as his cock size. Classy. She is a kitchen manager that moonlights as a lot lizard. This cheap slut doesn't get paid for it.

I had to report this, and ultimately, I got let go because of "too many managers." Yup, when I say she is a lying cocksucker, it's a very accurate assessment. She tried pinning the drunken slut behaviour on me. Yup, I dragged the staff member and forced his cock down your throat. Again, weak management and a poisoned work environment. Where the lying snitches get away with it all, we had a lot of turnovers for staff. Do you wonder why?

It was funny how the owner's other little favourite model employee was robbing him blind too. It's only $80,000. I found this out after I got let go. I will never get an apology and would never want to go back anyway.

This other favourite employee was also tickling the waitresses and making lurid comments on their bodies. Complete sexual harassment, and when the report I made went in, I get dismissed. All of this was put together and used against me even though numerous staff complained. Another kitchen manager showed up drunk and threatened the staff. He got treated better than I did.

Another lesson learned, and once again, goes back to the brown-nosing of management or the owner. It all goes to the tell-tale signs of a snitch. As you can see, a snitch is the most toxic element in any workplace. His special people could do no wrong. The right side does not always win. That shit hole does not deserve any further discussion.

*　*　*

In culinary, It's you on the plate. You want to represent yourself in a positive light. I had to intercept a special dish for a birthday. I still can't believe a grown man would cover a plate with excessive amounts of chocolate sauce and sprinkles for another adult—there was so much chocolate sauce on the plate that the cake was swimming in it. The candy sprinkles looked as if a small child got free reign over a box of sprinkles. Sprinkles for everyone! There had to be about two ounces of sprinkles on one piece of cake. How embarrassing.

I didn't want to hurt the cook's feelings, but that plate could not go out to a guest. I asked the server to take it to the server aisle, wait about a minute, and head back to us and say the guest did not like it and refused it. She agreed and did so.

"I'm sorry the guest would not accept this, and they want another one," she explained, playing along with my plan. Sometimes it is acceptable to lie cover someone's feelings. I wanted to ask, 'What the hell is that?' I took the high road. In this case, this cook was more receptive to constructive criticism versus being in his face.

"Okay, no problem, we will make another one," I said, taking it back. "Ok, we got a little heavy-handed on the sprinkles and sauce on this one," I stated.

I took out another platter and placed a cake in it. I grabbed the coulis and made a simple squiggly line with it. I then grabbed a strawberry and sliced it to fan it out. I placed the strawberry at the top end of the coulis. It was to make it look like a balloon. I placed pre-made happy Birthday chocolate leaning against the cake and put a birthday candle in the wide end of the wedge of cake.

"Keep it simple, and everyone is happy," I explained. "Not everyone likes sauce and sprinkles. We will save that for the sundae bar." He nodded in agreement. This guy worked hard everywhere he was assigned and made an error. It never happened again.

* * *

One coworker made the funniest mess ever. He went into the freezer to grab the frozen lasagna noodles and accidentally grabbed the puff pastry. I think it was because his glasses fogged up but still funny as hell.

Nine trays of lasagna got made with puff pastry. Nobody checked the box. When they were in the oven, all four layers rose and puffed out. They grew well above the two-inch hotel pan's capacity and slid into the oven itself. What a glorious mess it made with burnt sauce, cheese and puff pastry. That one is for the books.

* * *

The black vein on a shrimp is to be removed, with no exceptions. It is for waste removal from the shrimp. It's how they take a shit. Your guests do not want to give it a rim job.

I had to go back and devein over 200 pounds of shrimp because of this. Do the damn job right the first time. One of my friends and colleagues was helping me but was allergic to shrimp. There is nothing worse than watching the hives creep up his arm, and then you see it creeping up his neck.

I had to kick him out of the kitchen. "I love you and appreciate the help, but please get the hell out of here before I have to get out your EpiPen," I told him. Thankfully he left. That is not a task I want to do for a friend. Of course, I will do it when it comes to it, but it is best to avoid triggering that emergency.

We were working with Chef Joyce. I love her. She is a mentor and, like your slightly older sister, all rolled into one. We rocked that party for New Year's Eve. It went perfectly. The guests raved about the food we put out. Chef Joyce is a terrific leader and works with your strengths. Her team building is second to none. Her successful events and relations with her team speak for itself in the success. I loved working for her. She always had a positive atmosphere.

Chapter 15

We can discuss bad bosses for the rest of the book and probably write an entire series based on this subject. They wanted to make the operation more efficient with the excuses, complacent and dismissive management with training. The solution is to make the lazy staff work and be accountable. Nope. They decided to have Kaizen.

Kaizen is a Japanese philosophy of contestant improvements in efficiency and work practices. You will have a group of people from other areas and have little knowledge of what you do or how you watch you for up to 5 days, depending on the complexity of your location. They will make notes and observations on what you do and how you do it.

A spaghetti scribble tracks your movements by putting a pen on paper and tracing your steps as you walk. It makes a lovely toddler-like scribbling on the sheet that mimics your walking movements from here to there. I found it is a waste of time when the problems could easily be fixed by training the dullards.

The outcome of having five days of work was putting coloured duct tape on the counters to where things should go and having the utensils on carts more accessible and closer to your area. The carts disappeared before we opened. Time well wasted. The company paid these people to come up with this. It was a team of people for five days to come up with this. It sheds light on the fact that people waste a lot of time working in groups.

If you want to save time and make things more efficient, have people work alone. I have a friend who owns a cleaning business. It took half an hour extra to have one person clean an office building alone than two persons working together. Simply put, if you put two persons together, they will talk even if they hate each other. Eventually, they will communicate.

There is nothing more irritating than someone who knows absolutely nothing about your job telling you how you should do it. I would rather have a severe case of hemorrhoids than deal with the human version. I can deal with the itching and burning where I don't can't be sitting for an extended period and complete with some rupturing and bleeding.

Management is one to talk to. I have seen some severe inappropriate behaviour on their part too. They were leering, making inappropriate sexual comments on female guests: constant smoke breaks while their staff can't get theirs, favouritism including smoking with their friends. You can pass the kaizen bullshit around all you want. Fix the real problem. Team members can't do their job and make excuses for 15 years on why they can't. Talk about enabling.

Addressing the toxic culture in the workplace would be a great place to start. I had one workplace where the owner knew a particular employee was toxic but allowed her to continue the behaviour. She cried and put on the waterworks when she didn't get her way. She had no problem sabotaging your work or outright claiming it for herself. Sound familiar? She even did drugs on company time.

As a manager, I got hired to put things in line with costing and new products. The poison was deep in this place. They used many temporary employees, which should have been a warning that nobody makes it there. It was a revolving door. It's kind of hard to get the job done when you have to train new staff every few weeks and deal with outdated equipment.

It's funny how this poison pill sabotaged people's work and then went squealing on anyone and everyone she could. Staff quit because of her, and she stays employed. She is a known drug user, liar and shit disturber. It goes to the weak management thing. She even flashed her saggy tits at a male employee from her workstation. She stays employed. Disgusting. This ghetto trash is not even worth mentioning more than that. She worked later than everyone else and deliberately shorted orders daily. The owner knew, but it was my fault. Passing the buck and never dealt with the issue. Keep using temp agencies, pal. No one wants to work for you anyway.

The other one was super sensitive. She refused to taste any of her food because she was counting calories. She also liked to snitch on others for using profanity but did so herself. Today is all about double standards. Ban Pepe Le Pew, but Family Guy's perverts are just fine.

This place was taking whole canned tomatoes ad squishing them by hand to make chilli. Asinine and absurd. I had to make t this way the first time. I was squishing tomatoes by hand, and let me tell you, and it does not stay in the bowl. They squirt everywhere, making the kitchen look like a Jackson Pollock painting. It makes a fuck of a mess. That took an additional twenty minutes to clean up. I could not fathom who would be so stupid to put this practice into play. Are you kidding me? That was 50 minutes of my life I will never get back.

I quickly changed it to diced tomatoes, and the staff was upset because they had time-wasting half an hour squishing tomatoes by hand. Not only is it a waste of time, but it looks like shit. Do you like getting a whole squished tomato in your bowl? I don't, nor did some of the customers, because I got several sent back. They did not have an immersion blender for this either—what a shit show.

I put in 10 hour days and trained several temporary employees to be sabotaged and set up for failure. When the owner felt "I served my purpose"(The owner's exact words to me), I was dismissed on my birthday and given my job to his friend. They went right back to squishing whole canned tomatoes by hand. When you are stuck on stupid, you get stuck on stupid. They were called Touch of Class Catering. A touch of class, my ass. They should call it No Class Catering. It is more fitting.

"Oh, you are gone. You lost, loser. The circus is hiring. It's a better fit for you anyway," was a text I got from the poison pill.

"I will find something else quite easily. If you lose your job, You will have to wait for the strip club to lower their standards and have Meat Curtain Mondays. Then you can have your true calling where your skills lie. Sponsored by Arby's-we have the meats."

* * *

In food and beverage, I have heard some of the best insults and one-liners as well. I had to do a meeting with two servers who hated each other. One had a breast enhancement, and the other was a shorter feisty lady. I will give you a few exchanges. We will call them Sally and Sue.

"Nice boob job," said Sally.

"Than you. It's better than your flabby pancakes." shot back Sue.

"That's ok. Insult me all you want. It is better that you gave the customers something else to look at, and It takes attention off of your ugly face," replied Sally.

* * *

"I have a headache," announced Sue

"That's too bad. Have you tried cyanide capsules?" Asked Sally.

* * *

"Nobody takes me seriously in this place," complained Sue.

"Of course not. Your make-up matches a circus clown," replied Sally.

* * *

"I do a better job than you!" bragged Sue.

"Ok. Are we talking about fellatio? I'm ok that you have way more experience than I do." replied Sally.

* * *

"You are short and fat. I am better at this than you are," said Sue.

"The only thing you are better at is knowing your way around a mattress," shot back Sally.

* * *

Honestly, there should be some shows dealing with this subject on the Food network. Eatin' with the Creetins and Delusional Diner comes to mind—the fun I could have with this sort of creation. You will be able to put it on the Comedy channels too.

I mentioned now let's set up the parameters. Let's start with Eatin' with the Cretins. A show where we showcase some of the stupidest and most asinine orders and dishes we have ever been asked to make or have witnessed being made.

Our lovely Roast Beef Sushi would be a good contender. I have even heard of coffee with nine cream and nine sugar- syrup, anyone?

* * *

We could also use that for ridiculous complaints. It is incredible the levels some will stoop to try and get a free meal. In this case, it was one of my employee's aunt and uncle. They were a handful. It mainly was her—a real prize.

Here is how it went down. She came in and sat down with her husband; She ordered soup, and he had a salad. Wings were on order.

We delivered the soup and salad to their table, and they started to eat them right away. I gave them about 10 minutes and brought out the wings. She looked at me in disgust.

"I'm not paying for that," she said in a snotty voice.

"Fine. Then you are not getting it," I replied and took it back to the kitchen.

She bitched to the server they wanted their wings. So I brought them out again. Of course, it was the same ones as they were put back under the heat lamp. I am not putting up with a "Karen" and her shit.

"Here are your wings, again," I announced.

"Are those the same ones from a couple of minutes ago?" she asked.

"Yes, they are, and I am not remaking them. It's been less than 5 minutes." People like this are always looking to start their shit and are overly demanding.

"I want new ones." She demanded.

"Your steaks are already on, and since you asked for medium-well, there is plenty of time to eat these. They are still hot."

"Fine. Leave the wings here," she replied, and it was a 'fuck off' implied in her tone.

We gave her time to eat her wings and then held the steaks back until the empty chicken wing plates were removed and put in the dish area. I waited an extra minute and then sent the steaks to the table. You know she is going to find something to complain about as that's what Karens do. She didn't disappoint.

I went to check on the tables and made a round through the restaurant, ensuring guest satisfaction. As soon s I was in sight, she waved me over to the table. I, of course, went over right away.

"My steak tasted like it is spoiled," complained her husband. He, of course, already consumed more than half.

"Oh really, and you ate half of it. Have you ever tasted a spoiled steak before? You would not make it past the first bite, yet you managed to eat half of this one, so it can't be that bad," I replied. I was getting annoyed with these lying assholes.

"Try it for yourself," he insisted.

I went against the protocol and cut a small piece off the unused side. I took a bite. Of course, there is nothing wrong with it. These people like to bitch and moan and cause problems.

"It tastes fine to me. We turn our steaks over frequently and have not had one turn. We get them in twice a week," I replied as diplomatically as I could. I hate liars.

"Well, I want another one," he demanded.

"Of course you do," I shot back.

"And mine is overdone, and I want it replaced," she interjected. She, of course, ate more than 2/3 of it. Why am I not surprised?

"It will be a few minutes," I responded. I removed the plates and went back to the kitchen. My kitchen manager almost lost his mind.

"Are you fucking kidding me," he asked. He was pissed.

"Refire it and shut her up. I know she is a miserable bitch. Complain, complain, complain. That's what they do to try and get discounts and free stuff," I responded.

We redid the steaks, and since they consumed the sides, I refused to replace them. I brought out the steaks, and she looked at me in disgust.

"Where are the sides?" she demanded.

"You finished them, and I am not replacing them," I said firmly.

"What good is a steak without sides?" she protested.

"You ate them and complained about half-eaten steaks. We replaced them. Did you complain about your sides? No. So, therefore, they will not be replaced. You asked for steaks, and this is what I am delivering," I firmly replied.

"Ugh," she grunted in disgust. This broad is a total fucking bitch. I wanted to punch her fucking snotty, condescending, lying fucking face until it looked like ground beef. I hate fucking liars. This bitch would look good bleeding from the head and nose blood looking like jello.

I slapped the plate in front of her. Yes, it landed with a thud. Some people just don't know when to quit. They keep pushing their luck to see how far they can go and then play the victim when you let them have it—typical 'Karen" behaviour, and of course, I already thought this bitch would have plenty to say on Social Media just as any spineless keyboard warrior.

It came time to pay the bill. You know it was an issue. The bitch wants it for free,

"I said I wasn't paying for the wings." She protested.

"You ate them all, and yes, you are. I discounted the steaks 25% even though you ate half of the first ones and then decided to complain. I gave you new ones, and you ate all of those too." I said, digging in my heels.

"I'm not paying it," she protested.

"Fine, I will call the cops now. It's called restaurant fraud, and it is chargeable and convictable in court. You ate it, and you are paying for it. Deal with it." I shot back. I could feel the hairs on the back of my neck rise and a surge of adrenaline. I wanted to punch her fucking face. The bitch needs it.

You know she went on social media and trashed us. It goes without saying for Karens.

"So this just happened. I went to this local restaurant and had steak. They were terrible, and the manager refused to replace the meals. I have never met such an ignorant jerk of a manager. We left hungry and went home for toast."

What a lying bitch. I did not bother to respond. Trash gets no response, only banned from the page. The worse part is that she was one of my cook's aunts and is known for being a scammer, making me hate her no-class bitch ass even more. See why I hate liars?

* * *

My other favourite is when they eat everything and then want to get out of paying. Nope, You ate it; you are paying for it. Case closed. If you are running short on cash, stay home. I put a few exchanges in below.

"Are you the manager?" asked a male customer.

"Yes, I am. What can I do for you?" I replied.

"I'm not happy with this hamburger," he answered. Of course, there were two bites left, and the fries were gone as well.

"What seems to be the issue?" I asked.

"Well, I thought it was hand-packed, and I don't want to pay for it. Can you discount it?" He responded. I can not believe he asked this. I quickly grabbed a menu.

"Nowhere on this menu do we claim hand-packed burgers. You have two bites left, so I am not discounting it." I replied and showed him the menu.

"That's not good customer service." He replied.

"Well, you live in fantasy land. You ate it, and now you want it for free. It's not happening. There is a difference between a legitimate issue than one made up like yours, for example. You are paying for it." I told him, and I was getting annoyed with his loser.

"Well, if you don't, I won't be coming back," he tried desperately.

"It's a $5 burger. I'll dearly miss you," I shot back. You should have seen the look on his face. He was shocked he wasn't getting his way. Obviously, this loser pulls that shit regularly.

* * *

We had a tagline customers liked to use for everything to try and get their way in the buffet. It is pathetic. This exchange should sum that up.

"Excuse me but do you have and pearl onions?" asked the guest.

"No, I am sorry. We are out at the moment," I responded.

"Oh, but that is what I came for!" he whined. There it is. 'That's what I came for.'

"Seriously?! You came to a buffet for pearled onions?! You got to be kidding me." I could not help it. I hear that for every little thing. 'Oh, but that's what I came for.' I am sure you read that with the mockery it deserves.

"I'm not. I want pearl onions," he responded.

"Sorry to disappoint you, but for $22.95, I would be coming for a lot more than pearl onions," I responded with my voice dripping in sarcasm. He laughed. Yeah, that's right, you just agreed you are an idiot, and your comment is just plain asinine.

* * *

"Excuse me. I only eat plain custard for dessert. Do you have it?" asked one lady.

"Sorry, we do not. We have things that are custard-based such as cream pies. We have banana, chocolate or coconut," I replied.

"No thanks, I want plain custard," she insisted.

"That's eggs, milk, sugar and vanilla. I really can't think of a resort that serves that. It's used as a base for other things. The closest thing to that would be pretty much a vanilla pudding or like the pies I mentioned," I informed her.

"Well then, I will have to go somewhere else," she answered in a snotty tone. The best part is she already paid for the buffet. I love when they think they have the upper hand by threatening to leave. Bu-Bye.

"Let me know how it works out."

* * *

This order infuriated me. A ticket came in with one pound of wings. The server put "one sauce per wing." I just bout lost my mind. Modifications to the menu slow down service. In this case, it is fucking bullshit. I refuse.

"Who took this order?" I demanded.

"I did," answered one of our new servers.

"What the fuck is this?" I asked. "One wing per sauce? Are you kidding me?!"

"That's what she wants...."

"I don't give a shit. It is one sauce per pound. We are not wasting our time and tossing each one. Look around you. It's a busy kitchen. Do you think we have time for this shit? It's ridiculous. You can march out here and ask her what sauce she wants them tossed in. She can have 2 to dip, but she pays for the second one. Do not ever bring me this garbage again," I told her.

"it's customer service...."

"Don't you dare talk back to me! No restaurant does one wing in each sauce. The standard is one per pound. Now fix your mistake! Go!" I was getting pissed off now. That shit doesn't fly. She left and came back.

"Honey Garlic," she informed me.

"Much better. Thank you. There is service, and then there is ridiculous. Some like to take advantage. Use better judgment," I responded.

* * *

This next one was when I was a customer. I saw a cook come from the kitchen and give his friend a cake with a giant penis drawn on the plate in chocolate sauce. The dining room is not the place, and your line cook ass belongs in the kitchen. Case closed. I will not mention the name of the restaurants, as you can see, but these things need to be brought forward for immediate attention. It's okay to joke with your friends but not so your guests see it.

"Is there a manager on duty?" I asked my server.

"Yes," she replied.

"Go get them, please. It is nothing you did," I asked.

The manager came right over within minutes.

"What can I do for you?" she asked.

"Look at the table to your right and look at the plates. Tell me if that is appropriate," I asked.

She looked over and saw the plate and came right back. "Oh my goodness! Who brought that out?"

"It was one of your cooks. I can handle a joke, but when you bring that out in a family-style restaurant, it needs to be addressed," I replied.

"Oh, and I assure you it will be addressed immediately. Thank you for bringing this to my attention," said the manager before heading to the kitchen. She was appalled and should be.

* * *

Here's a reason why you should not sleep with your coworkers. One girl I worked with had no problem telling us how small a particular cook's penis was. She compared it to a cocktail weenie. It sounded like the guy had a micro. When your sexual partner is not happy with you, you become the subject of conversation and ridicule.

As an openly gay man, I have had a female co-worker ask me about certain parts of the male anatomy. She even said he was willing to experiment. His having made several homophobic slurs and gestures in my direction made this even more accessible. I was only too eager to help now.

I told her the concept of milking the prostate where fingers or a sex toy are inserted in his anus and stimulating the gland. There was nothing more fulfilling to know he was up to three fingers and liked it as well as the fact he asked for it regularly.

The even more fulfilling part was when he saw me talking to her, and I held up three fingers together as if ready for his next prostate session. He turned white as a ghost. You can't out cunt a gay man.

He waited until she was gone and came walking over to me. I waited and withheld my comments and let him talk first.

"You are friends with my girlfriend?" he asked.

"I am," I responded.

"Did she ask you about that technique?" he asked.

"She sure did, and once I found it was you, I had no problem helping out. You shouldn't make slurs. It turns out you like it too," I smiled and said to him.

"Yeah," he laughed. "Sorry about that. I won't do it again."

"No worries. Have a good one," I replied. He never made another slur again.

***

This one is a real gem. In the buffet, we had small braised mini ribs. The item got removed because of this incident. It could have been handled a lot better, but I will add my opinion to the situation. I was watching the manager getting cussed out about this item by a huge man. He was overweight and had his finger in her face. Putting your finger in my face is a massive no-no to me. It shows disrespect, and if you want my help, I suggest you use diplomacy and show some respect. It is a two-way street.

"Why would you put those on the menu. I didn't know the mini ribs had bones, and I almost choked!" This man was screaming in the manager's face. Well, let's look at the item. Ribs. Ribs are bones, and upon visually inspecting the item, you can see rib bones sticking out the ends.

"I'm sorry this happened…" she started to explain.

"Don't be sorry!! Fix it!! Put up a notice they have bones!!"

"I will. Again I am sorry this happened," the front-of-house manager replied.

Now let's look at it. To have this problem, this man stuffed his mouth full of ribs well beyond regular bites. He didn't even look at them. He stuffed his face, and upon chewing, I am surprised he took the time to chew it. He discovered they had bones, so because he can't admit that he is a glutton, it is now our fault because he stuffed himself so full and slowed down the feeding frenzy.

Ribs are bones, dumbass. It's right in the name—mini ribs. You almost choked? Really? Try taking regular bites and enjoy your food instead of trying to inhale it or swallow it whole like a python. It's not an eating competition. You have 75 minutes to eat, and all-you-can-eat is not an eating competition or a personal challenge. You almost choked? Slow the fuck down and take smaller bites and enjoy your food. Problem solved, fat ass.

* * *

Neil and Bob's friend became my supervisor. I could not imagine Hell being any worse. I got written up for using the restroom because I abandoned my work area while Neil and his crew could go for countless smoke breaks. I got written up for using my phone as a timer for pasta even though there were none to use. I used it as a watch and got it for that too. He made a video of an attractive patron wearing a short skirt and made several lude comments. Do as I say, not as I do. Hypocrite. I left that place because of it. He told the chefs that hired me were gone, and nobody had my back. I was going to pay now.

Thanks to his group and his shit, I had a breakdown and was misdiagnosed with Bipolar 2. It took five years, $2,000 out of pocket, to get rid of it. I lost a lot of opportunities and nearly had a seizure coming off the medications I was taking. It is not cool to fuck with someone's mental health. Do I forgive them? Not a chance in Hell. I got diagnosed over the phone, and I found out that it was unethical to do so. I am still working on a resolution over that.

He applied elsewhere, and let me tell you how many enemies he has. I would not recommend him to anyone.

* * *

We had one customer who ate for 7 hours straight. It is appalling. I get you are hungry but to consume that much food is very unhealthy. Yes, he was huge. He could not fit in a booth. He had to have a chair at the end of the table and have his rascal there to accommodate him.

It is sad to see guests in this state. Morbid obesity is a bad thing and can have serious health effects. These health effects are osteoarthritis, heart disease, stroke, type 2 diabetes, sleep apnea, reproductive problems, cancers, gallstones, hyperventilation, and metabolic syndrome.

Unfortunately, this person died early. Obesity can shorten your life. Yes, I made an insensitive comment in the previous story. However, please take care of your health: Diet and exercise. We covered the lying fad diets, which are nothing more than a cash grab. Let's look at tried, tested and true methods.

Eat more fruits and vegetables. In a buffet, start t the salad bar. Load up on fruits and vegetables.

Eat smaller meals. Proteins are harder to break down.

Count calories. There are lots of free apps out here to count them. I treat mine like cash. Look for the better deal. For example, a bag of potato chips is 240 calories. Popcorn is 80 calories, and a light beer is 110 calories. So I can have popcorn and a light beer for less than a bag of potato chips: winner, winner. That is 50 calories saved.

I was eating mindfully. Make better choices and watch what you eat. When I quit smoking, I would eat a veggie tray I made at home. When I was full, I stopped, and it was a minimal calorie intake.

Limit saturated fats, trans fats and refined sugars. Breaded chicken breasts around 200 calories, whereas a boneless and skinless breast, is around 110 calories. Better choice. That is 80 calories saved for later. Your mission: have leftover calories and feel full. Save the calories, and then treat yourself later on. One cup of berry ice cream is 150 calories. Treat it like cash. Make better choices—more bang for the buck.

The best exercises are running, jogging, swimming, cycling, and swimming. Be active and drink more water. The apps give you credit for these activities.

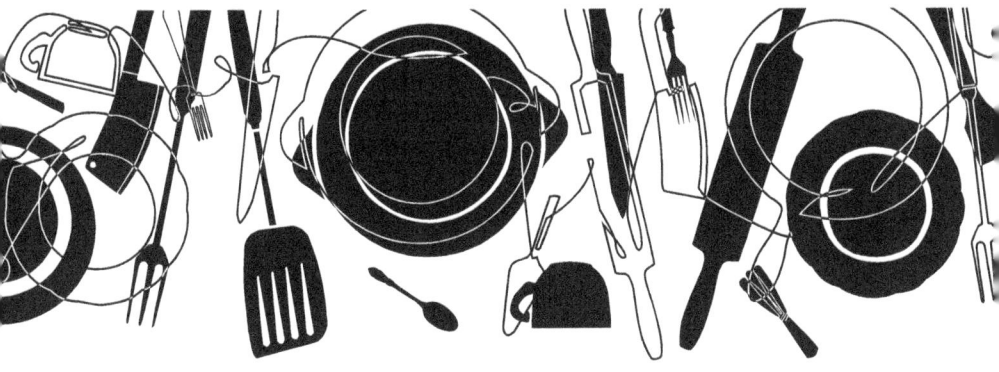

Chapter 16

For fun, we will address the Delusional Diner. I always get a kick out of it. Usually, a leftist thinks business owners have bottomless pockets and have all kinds of money from their operation.

These people also don't think the rich pay any taxes at all. Check out your country's tax codes. I can assure you they do. However, it comes into play like everyone else, where your deductions and operation expenses are handled. It is all about cash flow in a business.

If you recall the costing exercise we did earlier with the burger and fries, you can see how prices are made for the menu. Remember the 30-30-30-10 split? 30% Food Costs, 30% Labour Costs, 30% rent, utilities, insurance, etc. and the last 10% ideally should be profit. For example, the burger costs $3.51 to make it. It is not far off at the time this is written. Food costs will fluctuate based on market prices, so keep that in mind based on seasons, product availability, and other fuel prices.

That is another one that gets me. These people expect the owners and drivers to suck it up when price increases to have the lowest price on the consumer end. It doesn't work that way in anything. So let's do the flip side. The cost of living is always going up. Suck it up and keep your wages low. That doesn't work either.

In economics, it is all connected. When costs go up, so do prices. Case closed. Do you want a raise? Sure. We all do. There is a price to that raise. It costs the employer more to pay you. You can not always stick it to the customer either, as you will not have them if you keep doing it. Nobody likes a price increase, but it is a fact of life.

Food companies will hide the price increase in smaller packages at the grocery store. For example, a soup was 12 oz and now is 10 oz, but no price increase on the shelf. They raised the price by 20 % by giving you less. A particular chicken restaurant decided to cut their standard chicken from the traditional 9-cut chicken we use in the food industry to 12-cut. The price of chicken did not change, but you get less. The reality is a 33 % price increase. 12/9 is 1.33, so it went up 33 %.

So to give you that raise, there will be some cost-cutting or price increases. The employer may change the 2-ply bathroom tissue to 1-ply, reducing the "free" items you enjoyed in your workplace or removing them altogether. Everything has a price. Nothing is free. In other places, you may see automation and self-checkouts. The employer may lay off those persons and eliminating their jobs for your raise or other items instead of raising prices. $15 an hour at a full-time rate of 40 hours per week is $31,200 per year.

New hires may have a second-tier wage system versus what you currently have in manufacturing. This does happen. It is to cut costs. You cannot stick it to the consumer constantly. It is always called corporate greed by the misinformed. In one aspect, there may be truth to it but realize everyone gets a piece of the pie.

There is no such thing as a perfect system, but the reality is the entry-level person usually takes the hit. No CEO or upper manager will reduce their earnings to save the dishwasher or the cashier any more than the plant manager will take a pay cut to protect the most junior employee from a layoff. Ask yourself this- are you willing to take a pay cut to save someone else's job? The chances are very high on the No side. You will dearly miss them, won't you? If you are not willing to do so, you should not expect someone else to. You deserve that raise; why would you give it up?

In food and beverage, you may see reduced waitstaff or counter service only. There are lots of ways to reduce costs, but eventually, it comes to price increases too. You see price increases at the grocery store, so you adjust. The same thing happens in business and politics.

I will be careful with this one. Note that I am not taking sides so that it will be generalized. I hear some say the government has money. This is false. It is your money. The government collects money from you to pay for the services we need. When they overspend the money they collected through taxes, we have a deficit. We are in debt. Tax dollars are not a limitless supply, just like your income. Raising taxes takes money out of your pocket.

You can not tax people to prosperity by taking more and more of their money. That is a trip to the poor house. That is not prosperity. Taking ore of your money does not make you prosperous. You have less money. The one that kills me is a rebate program on tax. They try and sell it to you that you are getting a cheque. Here's the reality, you paid a lot more than the rebate you are getting. I can take $100 from you and give you back $90 all day long as a rebate. Enjoy your rebate. You lost money. There is no such thing as "free money." Mousetraps are full of free cheese. There's a price to that, isn't there?

How does the government try to balance the budget? What does the government do? Either raise taxes or cut services. They cut services and reduce the things we do not need or the things they don't think we need. Again, there is no perfect system, and the cuts are not always where they need to be. How much tax do you want to pay?

How much price increases are you willing to put up with for the things you enjoy before you go elsewhere? If you are in that business with constant price increases, the cost is your job. Raise your prices too much, too often; the customer is gone.

I got a little off track so let's get back on track. That was necessary to shed light on the subject. The delusional diner can pay your employees $20 an hour and keep a burger and fries at $5 and beer at $1. It is an outlandish impossibility just based on the costing formulas alone. You will be a broke ass in no time. As an owner, kiss your house, car and relationship goodbye.

Consumers like to bitch and moan, as do employees. It's human nature. We all want nice things but don't want to pay for them at full price. You can't have 1950s prices in the 2020s. Ten cents for a hamburger? Not happening. I will give you a slice of tomato for ten cents if you are lucky at today's prices.

The bottom line is you cannot have high wages and low prices. It is an Impossibility. Specials are run to bring customers in, encourage spending, and spend a little more on something else. Preferably something with a nice profit margin like an appetizer or a drink. It is like that in Las Vegas. Cheap rooms or free rooms encourage you to spend your time there and that you will gamble a little more. Get your gift? Sure, you are not just going in for a gift; the odds are very high that you will play one of their table games or slot machines.

Ever get a free movie at the cinema? Yeah, they make minimal off of that. Pennies. They make their money on the concession stands. They want you to buy soda and popcorn.

Those prices are higher because movies don't make money. The box office takes that along with the studio. Snacks they do, they get a volume discount and sell it at a higher price. That is what pays for the staff and the bills. When you smuggle in outside food, you are potentially hurting someone else's job. You would not like it if someone came into your work and did that, so don't do it to anyone else.

A good owner or manager has to manage costs. Labour is a cost. It is the highest cost in food and beverage operations. When it is slow, a good manager will cut you and end your shift early. Of course, they have to follow labour laws in your jurisdiction as per minimal shift times. I will keep you for that and then send you home. If it is slow, it is extra cleaning time. If you don't want to do that, you can voluntarily leave, which overrides the laws again depending n jurisdiction. It was your choice.

Customers may want those prices too. It is not happening, and I even had a neighbour that convinced her husband it is cheaper to eat out than cook at home. That was also because someone else was paying. Wow, talk about delusional and a good hustler.

At home, you are not paying staff to wait on you and cook your food. Restaurant food costs may be lower; however, the rest gets costly. Those other costs like labour are why a burger costs $12 and up. Nobody works for free. When you eat out, you are paying wages and the other costs too. It's all part of the costing formula, even in the retail business. Store space and labour costs are real.

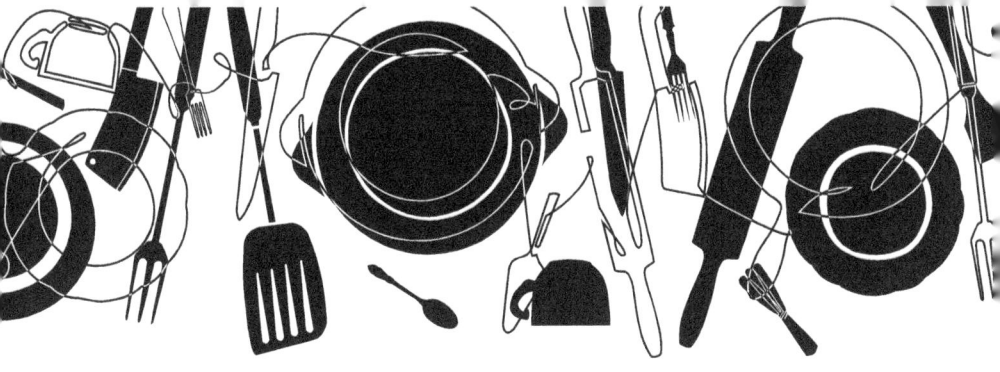

Chapter 17

I could do days with the material on Eatin' with the Creatins. There is no shortage of stupidity in food and beverage. It's right there in the name. F & B. Fucking Bullshit. It can be fun, but there is always someone who enjoys being a total dick like anything. Stay home and let people have their enjoyment.

In this business, you will see the good, the bad and the ugly. There is always something to get a laugh out of it. My chef friends turned in some gems for our entertainment, so that I will throw those in now. Again, we will not name places and establishments. Idiots are everywhere and unavoidable.

Cruise ships have elegant food, and once again, the public is not well informed on food. In this case, this chef was carving a beef hip.

"Excuse me, is that lamb?" asked a guest. That would be a very scary lamb if that were the case. Yikes.

"Oh my god. I can't handle the stupidity. Ma'am, you are fucking stupid. It's a beef hip. Do you know the size of a lamb? I can't handle the fucking stupid. Fuck you!" he shot back. The chef took off his apron and stormed out of the dining room.

He went right out the doors to the deck and jumped off the ship from 6 floors up right into the Mediterranean Sea. The boat had to slow down and circle. Man overboard alarm was called, and luckily, he survived the fall and was rescued. This poor soul had mental health issues and needed a break as well as some professional help.

* * *

The same chef told me how he drank Wiessen beer in Switzerland, and apparently, it gives you wicked gas and nasty farts. Now, this is how it played out. My friend drank the beer the night before.

My friend was doing prep work by himself and had a bit of a gas problem. Like anyone else, he let it slip out. Silent and deadly. Fire one. Fire two and fire three.

"Oh my god, what is that smell?!" shrieked a female coworker.

"Oh my god. That's sulphur!"

"There is a leak. It isn't good. We have to evacuate the building!"

The building was immediately evacuated in an orderly fashion, and a hazmat team was called to investigate the alleged Wilder (sulphur) leak. Of course, they came with the sirens on. I would not have been able to contain the laughter. I cleared a bus before, but this is a prize winner. This one has to be a record for the smelliest farts ever.

He could not tell the truth. Too embarrassing. I can relate, but luckily hazmat was not called in my case. Maintenance was called for me for my ass gas. That was embarrassing enough. I never owned up to it either, nor did he. Would you? Probably not.

* * *

The Chef kept finding melons with holes in them. He could not figure out why. The Chef got a closed-circuit camera system installed in the kitchen and walk-in coolers. There was no reason for it, as melons are not typically hollowed out for any purpose.

Upon further investigation and viewing the surveillance footage, an employee was microwaving the melons with holes in them and pleasuring himself with them to full climax inside the melons, right in the kitchen and under the surveillance cameras. Produce porn. That's a new one. I am wondering if he gets excited in the produce department at the grocery store now. Nice melons.

Cucumbers are great; they stay hard for a week. Jumbo carrots are more rigid apparently and than the eggplant emoji, which raises questions about that. Has this person tried eggplant in that way? Good lord and that much girth. It makes you wonder.

In the kitchen, we will make inappropriate jokes with produce. It happens if it looks like a dick, there will be a joke. It's just what happens in a kitchen. We can be crude with the jokes.

* * *

The bigger guy always has to pull the big pecker contest. It is always entertaining to watch the exchange. The jokes are always good.

"Hey, you know what they say about small guys, right," asked Chef Dickhead to his shorter Sous Chef.

"What is that ?" asked the Sous Chef.

"Well, I am 6 Foor 2, and things are always proportional," said pompous ass Chef Dickhead.

"So you are saying you have a bigger dick than I do. Is that what you are saying?" asked the Sous Chef.

"That is exactly what I am saying," answered Chef Dickhead.

"Okay, I will tell you what. You can pull it all out, and I will put out just enough to beat you and embarrass you. How does that sound?" replied the Sous Chef. "You can begin any time." Chef Dickhead turned beet red. He was speechless and walked away.

* * *

A cook whose job was to peel the garlic and seed chilli peppers went on a restroom break. He was pleasuring himself but did not wash his hands properly after handling the chilis. He was sent to the hospital with second-degree burns on his member. That one is for the books, for sure. Never whip your willy after handling chilis of any kind. Always wash your hands before touching your privates.

* * *

I had a supervisor in one of my outlets who had an irritating voice and was not knowledgeable about the menu. She went into a fridge and left her phone outside. On both sides of the refrigerator, there was a shelving unit full of dry goods. The broom slipped and fell between the shelves and got wedged, keeping the refrigerator door from opening. The poor front-of-house manager got trapped inside the walk-in cooler for over an hour. I went on my lunch break, and I have no idea how that happened. What a terrible freak accident. Who am I kidding? It was me bitch. Your voice is like a chicken on helium. It was the best hour of silence ever. Isn't it amazing how I passed it off as an accident and got away with it?

* * *

A chef working in Isreal in a kosher kitchen had a religious person checking that the meat and dairy never crossed the line marked on the floor. He decided to make a blasphemous double downer. He made a bacon cheeseburger. He sat on the line drawn on the floor in the walk-in cooler. A bacon cheeseburger is very non-kosher, and the religious inspector broke down and cried as he didn't know how to handle the situation. The result was a written warning. According to the Chef, it was the best written warning he ever received.

* * *

Here's a funny one you can pull on your friends. When the Italians first came to America, they noticed that some were larger and eating cakes and pastries. The term MAngiacake was born. It translates into "Cake Eater." It is for someone who is not of Italian descent.

So, like a good joke. Tell your friends that they have to try the fantastic dessert at the local Italian restaurant. It's called Mangiacake. It is the best you have ever had. Make sure you are present when the joke plays out. The waiter should die laughing.

* * *

At an around the world buffet, a lady piled her plate full of nachos and then proceeded to load up on wasabi.

"Excuse me, ma'am, that is not guacamole. It is wasabi," informed the Chef on duty.

"II know the difference, and if I want 20 pounds of guacamole, I m going to take it! It's all you can eat!" she snapped back.

When she got to her table, she looked right at the chef with a loaded spoon of wasabi and placed it on the nacho chip. She even dared to shoot him the finger before shoving it in her mouth.

She turned to beat red and started choking. This Chef ran to the walk-in cooler because he was laughing so hard. It was instant Karen karma.

I can relate to this as I took my sister-in-law to a buffet and said the more wasabi, the better on a piece of sushi. She put a large spoonful on the first piece of sushi. I swear I saw the colour of her face change to bright red and her ears too before she spits in the napkin. It was the best punch in the arm I ever got in my life.

* * *

A particular hotel had its chef pose with a "fresh-caught tuna" and paid the "fishermen" for their daily catch. A tourist chef went to check out the tuna, and it was frozen—a complete sham.

Dishonesty gets you nowhere. Eventually, the truth always comes out. Lies are ultimately exposed over time.

* * *

One of my friends was good at insults. This is one of his gems. "Why don't you go and take a bath in Gynecure, and then maybe you will stop being an irritating cunt."

* * *

"Oh my god, she is so stupid. The only way I will be able to communicate with her is if I learn dolphin squeak." Another one of my friend's gems.

"Dolphins are cute and trainable with fish. The only way to train her is with a cattle prod and high voltage. Please do not make me hate dolphins. Doing that with her will do it." I replied.

A chef was taking their first day in Africa, where the staff at the hotel figured it was best to slaughter their beef indoors. They had no idea the cow would run around like that, spraying blood everywhere in the hotel after having its throat slit. A live slaughter in the kitchen is probably not the best way to advertise the freshest beef.

Could you imagine seeing that from the dining room where your kitchen doubles as an arbiter or a slaughterhouse? Neither can I. Butchering animals in your kitchen is a lousy judgement call.

* * *

It is crucial to never piss someone off with access to your toothbrush and food at a particular resort operation. However, the General manager's toothbrush was used to clean his toilet in his office. His teeth were as white as his porcelain. It is probably not a good decision to reduce staff hours and benefit eligibility for those who clean your office and restroom.

Also, when you condescend to your culinary staff and demand unrealistic items and insult them on their work ethic and time management through unjust disciplinary measurements, it is probably not a good idea to have them make your meals. When you provide the cheapest and toughest cuts of meat, you should not expect the tenderness of the most expensive cuts of meat.

Special seasonings and treatment may happen under your plan. After all, it would be best if you were the first to try the special recipe. The mashed potatoes may be creamier than usual, as well as a special blend of herbs and spice added to the culinary offerings of the day. The staff you have decided to insult and criticize may forget to wash their hands before returning from the restroom when they make your food. The same team member may or may not have a runny nose due to the allergies to your over-priced perfume. Bon appetite, bitch.

You expect the same staff you hope to rally behind your back and ensure you have a positive environment and exceptional service. You decided to criticize, demean and condescend to the team. Have no fear; the team has your best interest in mind when making your meals.

You have to watch when the sweat drips right off their nose, or it gets so hot the nose becomes runny. Do you know how much blood, sweat and tears go into making meals for people like yourself in the micromanagement leader-shit team?

* * *

This one needs to be told as well. It was a busy Saturday night, and the pass was full of plates. I was the expediter and was working from the server aisle. I had three food runners and seven wait staff. There was no excuse for the pass to be that full of plates.

One of the cooks kept pushing the plates.

"Stop pushing the plates. I don't have any more room over here," I told him calmly. He kept pushing them.

"Stop pushing the plates!" I ordered him. Too late. A bunch crashed and broke in the server area where we kept the garnishes and sauces. The entire line had to be thrown out because broken plates got into them all. Haste makes waste.

"I told you to stop pushing the fucking plates! When I say Stop, you fucking stop! You wasted this entire table, and it has to be remade! The whole line has to be thrown out and redone here because you don't fucking listen! If you fuck up like this again, you are fired! Now clean it up and make the order you fucked up top priority!" I was livid. "When someone says Stop- You fuckingStop!!" I screamed at him.

This blunder cost us five entrees and a full soup plus the sour cream, salsa, gravy, and garnish. Listen to your manager. Listen to your chef.

Chapter 18

I did work in assisting culinary students, and it was part of their internship and training. It bothers me that others in the industry would teach them bad habits. Not only is this a Health and Safety issue, but it is very reckless as well. Short cuts get you to the emergency room. I had one student who was assigned to clean the meat slicer. When I got over to him, he held a cleaning rag on top of the spinning blade with the blade setting wide open.

"What are you doing?" I asked him.

"What does it look like? I am cleaning the slicer," he answered with a smart-ass tone.

"Who the hell taught you to do that way? That is reckless and irresponsible. " I replied.

"My chef."

"Your chef is an idiot, and I will gladly tell him that to his face. Please turn it off now and unplug it. I will show you the proper way. One false move like that, and you are going to the hospital." I informed him. He turned off the unit and unplugged it as instructed. Good. I can't believe someone would teach such a reckless and dangerous way to clean a slicer.

Rather than go through the conversation I had with the student, I will put the instructions in my own words on cleaning a slicer. There are other maintenance items for sharpening the blade and oiling the unit. However, the issues at hand are proper cleaning and Health and Safety.

HOW TO CLEAN A MEAT SLICER.

1. Unplug the unit.
2. Close the blade and set it to zero.
3. Wear a cut-resistant glove.
4. With the gloved hand and a wet cloth, remove the food residue.
5. Remove the blade sharpener, blade guard, and handle.
6. Place the removed parts in a sink with hot soapy water and wash them, rinse and sanitize and allow to air dry.
7. Wash the unit with hot soapy water according to the manufacturer's recommendations. Always wear cut-resistant gloves when doing so.
8. Use a food service-recommended sanitizer after the unit is cleaned and rinsed.
9. Reassemble the parts to the slicer.
10. Plug the unit back in, and it is ready for use.

* * *

Along with the slicer issue, which I have seen many improper methods used, knives improperly used is another one I always raises its ugly head. Do you remember Jim from earlier? I had another student who had most of the skills right. The only problem was he was drawing the knife towards himself. His cuts were significant, and he used the wet towel under his board. It was the knife moving towards himself. The counter was low, and the knife blade was getting too close to his leg for my liking.

"Please cut away from your body, not towards it," I asked him.

"But, I was shown this way by the previous chef," he protested.

"Ok, but if that knife slips and it is going into your leg. You have a major artery in your leg, and you can bleed out in minutes. We are several miles away from the nearest hospital. I do not pick on people.

And you have another important body part nearby too. Sharp objects should always be away from that too. I would not want to see you get hurt, and if it is avoidable, the best practice is to avoid it. Push the blade away from you. If the knife slips, it is going to the middle of the table. Let's practice that movement," I explained.

"Thank you for thinking of my safety," he replied. He started working on the motion of forwarding cuts.

"Any time. Work is supposed to be a good and fun environment. Accidents are not fun," I said.

"Noted," he replied. I liked this young man. I wanted to help him out. He was always pleasant to be around, and he could make pizzas with speed and accuracy better than anyone else in the restaurant. He was only 17.

* * *

I usually had the task of training someone on the meat slicer for operations as well. Some people do not listen at all, and it is frustrating. They will tell you they got it so that you will shut up and go away. I find this insulting because there is a lack of respect once they feel you are 'old.' I find this insulting. With age comes experience and knowledge. When we have these conversations, it is a pass it off and pay-it-forward moment. You have not reached the level of Chef, and you are in training.

Skipping the conversation on the subject, I will again give the proper instructions for operating a meat slicer.

I showed him to use it properly and asked if he understood. He, of course, answered "yes" within 5 minutes; he was on his way to the hospital as he took off part of his finger.

He was dismissive and didn't give a shit about the instructions he was to follow. A snot nose know-it-all. Good to see it works out for people like that. It is aggravating when they have it in their head that you are old, stupid and senile. I just turned 40 and have lots of experience to share. Some are not as receptive and get what they get. In this case, a trip to the emergency room for failure to follow instructions.

The exact instructions are in the owner's manual, but I m glad you know everything, asshole.

Of all the professionals I know, this is not an isolated incident. It happens all the time. Who the hell do these kids think they are? I have had general managers believe the same and have no respect for the trade. That is coming too- a management team I despise. Lying pieces of shit. You watched a cooking show, good for you. I am glad you know everything.

HOW TO OPERATE A MEAT SLICER.

1. Put the machine in manual mode.
2. Lift the pushed and place the food in the carriage.
3. Turn on the machine.
4. Set blade to desired slice thickness
5. Use the handle to slide the carriage up and down and keep your hands away from the blade.
6. All the food to fall on slicer base
7. Transfer sliced meat to a tray or pan.

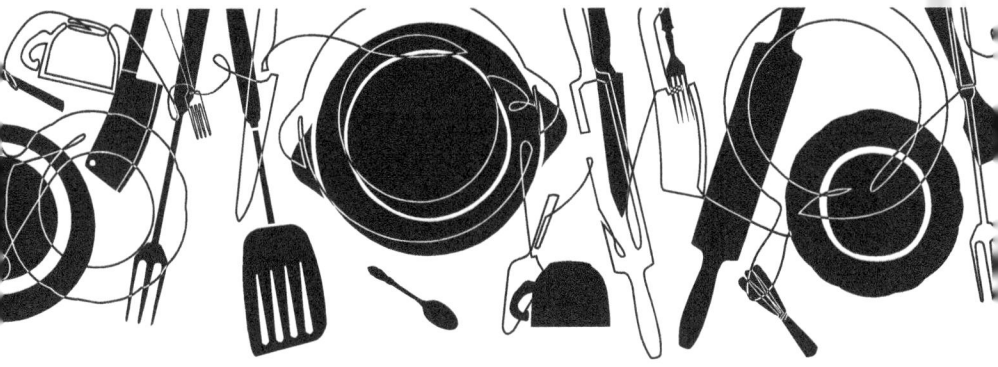

Chapter 19

I worked with many chefs over the years—some I love and others not so much. I had one, in particular, I had very little respect for when I was working as a banquet chef. He was the sous chef and quite the condescending jerk. Chef Steve. Yes, It is his real first name. We were actually in the same culinary program. I had a higher GPA and more experience. He led through intimidation and bullying. He was rude and condescending. I have very little to no respect for people like that. I already dealt with a group of them. So the hell I will respect this loser.

I did my best to keep my answers short with him and worked well with the other chefs. I made sure I was paired with them instead. The more I was away from this asshole, the better. I disapprove of his condescending and belittling remarks. He didn't give assignments and tasks effectively. If the instructions were not present, he gave you more condescending comments, and he would even put his hand in your face. Steve is a no-class cunt.

I was working by myself with him on duty one morning. He looked at me and then walked away. He had something on his mind. He was pacing and looking at me. He wants to talk. This should be good.

"May I see you in the office for a minute?" he asked me.

"Sure," I answered and followed him to the office.

"Close the door," he instructed. This should be good. I closed the door,

"I want you to start respecting me. You clearly don't, and I want it to stop," he said frankly.

"Okay then. Let's get it out in the open, Steve…." I started.

"That's Chef Steve to you," he said, trying to push his authority. I rolled my eyes. He glared at me. I smirked back and gave a huh under my breath.

"Well, as I was saying, Steve. I have the same credentials as you and am more experienced than you. If you want my respect, you can give some my way, and I will return it. You have none for me, and I sure as hell am not giving you any in return. It's a two-way street, pal," I informed him. The look on his face was priceless. I don't give a shit if you outweigh me or not. I am lean, and you have a spare tire. I will not provide this shithead with an inch of ground.

"You dare talk to me like that?" he challenged me.

"Yup, do you want the conversation to continue? Do you want to talk about respect in the Executive Chef's office? I would love to bring it up in front of him. Do you want to?" I challenged him back. He sat in his chair like a deer in the headlights.

"I want your respect," he said again.

"And again, you get what you give, pal. Are we done here? Any other chef that comes in here you address as Chef. Until I get the same, you are Steve," I told him frankly. I turned and left him in the office. He can fuck right off. Respect is earned. You cannot bully it out of someone. It does the opposite. You lose more respect for that person.

I did bring forward the conversation to the Executive Chef. I don't keep secrets when it comes to workplace breakdowns. That son of a bitch does not intimidate me. He can bang his chest and stomp his feet all he wants about respect, and he can fuck right off. I will roll my eyes even louder. Show me some courtesy, and I will do the same. Until then, fuck you.

Jerks like that never last. No one likes a bully. There is another thing I do. I always roll up my sleeves and clean with my crew. If you have a chef that doesn't clean and thinks you are their bitch, you have a big problem. A chef that doesn't clean needs to get their ass in the dish room or pot room. I find it humbling and a team-building thing. I have way more respect for a chef that cleans with their crew than one who doesn't.

I clean and scrub my kitchen with my crew daily. I will cook my staff food too. I have worked with chefs who think I am foolish for doing so. Here's my reasoning: When someone cooks for you, it shows they value you and what you do. I appreciate what my crew does, and if they are busy and have not eaten, I will make it for them. It is a thank you for a job well done. I get more respect and appreciation from my staff that way and when I clean with them. Lead by example.

I always think of the Executive chef that shook my hand that was filthy from scrubbing pots. That is a man I still respect to this day. That's a Chef. That's a leader. He never demanded respect from me. He earned it right then and there. All of my dealings with him were pleasant, and I most certainly respect him. He treated me with respect and like I mattered to him. He appreciated the job I did for him, so you're damn right I respect him.

Steve doesn't get it and never will. That makes him weak. Steve has no respect coming his way. He thinks he is King Shit, and everyone else is shit on the bottom of his shoes. A condescending and belittling jerk off. Steve is a weak leader. He demands to be called chef. Not from me, but I will gladly call him an asshole. He earned that. Did he ever.

It was not the first time I have run into this, and it won't last. You can not negotiate respect or mandate respect. You earn it. There is no way I will respect a liar, a talentless hack or a kiss ass and most definitely not a snitch.

*　*　*

I was also working part-time at a retirement home to help out. I have a lot of respect for those who work in this sector. It is a thankless job. You have many special diets, pureed food and sometimes meddlesome helpers or family who think they are making the best decisions for the elderly.

Some seniors can be a handful, but they earned it. I did my best. This home was smaller and a lot of fun. I liked the staff and the residents. The residents were fun, and I would introduce myself to them when I finished cooking. It's a nice gesture. I tried to make them at home. They are home.

You get a specific budget per person to feed everyone, and I tried to make the best of it. I am not going to name the places, but I will call some of the behaviour. One resident was just a comedian. He would run bare ass down the hallway in the morning with a sock covering his member. He would run up to the nurses and ask if they saw anything they liked, giggle and run back to his room. It was pretty humorous. He was harmless, just having fun.

He liked simple things. He had dementia, and I still remember his food orders after these years. Breakfast was two eggs over hard with two pieces of soft bacon and two whole-wheat toast lightly toasted and lightly buttered. Lunch, he liked peanut butter and strawberry jam sandwich with an occasional bowl of soup. Dinner, he enjoyed his two eggs over hard with his toast and fruit for dessert. His wife was just happy and would eat whatever you put down in front of her. I was despondent when he passed away.

Another resident was very particular when it came to her food. She was a sweet lady until it came to her meals. She liked her English muffins for breakfast. She had two of them. You could not tear them. She wanted them cut perfectly in half, toasted twice as our toaster did not toast them to her liking. She liked lots of butter, not margarine. They had to come with two peanut butter and two raspberry jam. If she talked to her best friend, who she sat with daily, they went cold, and you made them again for her.

There was one day she kept talking to her friend, and the order got remade four times. I was losing my mind. Yes, five orders of English muffins went out to her. I think she was off her rocker that day. That woman wastes more food. One more time, and I swear I was going to have to kill her.

Her sandwich had to come from the middle of the loaf of bread, and her soup had to be hot, or she would tell you to take your stale ass bread and shove it up your fucking ass. If you didn't get it right, she would tell the dietary aids to fuck off and go for fast food. She was a feisty lady but as sweet as can be outside of the dining room.

She gave me a big hug on my last day. She was a lovely lady and funny as hell. I admired her honesty and feistiness. She even thanked me for putting up with her shit in the dining room—her exact words.

"I like you. You took it in stride. Did you notice I hardly did it anymore?" she asked me.

"Yes, I did," I answered.

"I asked who was cooking, and if it was you, I left it alone. You always went out of your way initially, and I knew you tried, so you earned my respect. You are good, and I liked how you made my plates special. I stopped complaining when you did it."

"Thank you. You are a sweet lady, and I'm glad to have met you," I replied. She gave me a hug and a small kiss on the cheek. I was moving on to another sous chef position. Some people leave a mark on you, and you never forget their order. I just hope that the rest of her life was enjoyable. I like to think she is still around tormenting the staff for her entertainment. Give them shit, Cheryl. Her real name.

* * *

I know I just jumped a bit, but the staff was fun. In hindsight, I should have stayed at this one. The staff was great and not a bunch of pathetic snitches like the last one. If we had an issue with someone, we talked it out. A lot of times, your issues are misunderstandings. My afternoon co-worker was a riot. She made me laugh.

The food budget in these places is tight. Generally, it is under $7 per senior per day for food. You have to get creative and utilize what you can and not waste anything. Institutional cooking is not like anything else. You are cooking for survival, not the wow factor for paying customers.

The homes try and create a restaurant experience for the residents, but you are given cheaper meat cuts as the budget allows. With that budget, you are not getting Prime Rib or filet mignon. You are getting inside or outside rounds for beef which are tougher in texture.

For chicken, you can bet lots of chicken quarters, including legs and thighs. There are many instant cake mixes, cookies, ice cream, instant puddings, frozen fruit pies like apple pie and jello for dessert. Cakes are decorated with oil-based whip topping because, naturally, whipping cream is more costly.

Vegetables will be frozen and rarely fresh unless in season. Fruit cups, pudding cups will be rare as instant puddings are cheaper. It is usually apples, oranges, bananas, strawberries and some melons when the prices are lower.

Salads like pasta, potatoes are an excellent starch substitutes, and usually, the meals include rice or potato or pasta. Pasta and tomato sauce is a cheap and filling meal with salad and garlic bread. The meals are delicious, working with the budget restraints.

Any leftover meats are used for soup for lunch within a couple of days. I never used the leftover meat from the night before. For example, if they had chicken cacciatore for dinner, they are not getting chicken noodle soup for lunch. They will know it is leftover chicken. I would do a bean and bacon, tomato, cream of broccoli or vegetable soup to throw them off.

The best chefs use their leftovers appropriately. Leftover chicken can be used in so many ways. Chicken salad, pasta salad, soup, pot pie, lasagna, stir fry, and fajitas, a la king, to name a few.

Any protein can be utilized in many ways. If I mention beef or pork, you can probably come up with several on your own. I will say a minimum of ten ways off the top of your head.

You do it at home. You will not discard half a roast beef at home, so it will not happen at a retirement home. It will be used for another meal. The trick is to do it in a way they don't know it is leftovers. You could try this tactic with children. They hate roast beef, but like fajitas, you know what to do. Cut in thin strips and toss it in Mexican seasoning with sauteed peppers and onions. Now you are the hero. The soup companies have lots of great ideas too. It makes a cheap and fast meal the family will enjoy.

Well run senior's homes will have plenty of sauce mixes, at least 3 or 4 kinds of pasta, rice, pasta sauces, stir fry sauces, barbecue sauces, potatoes, basic baking needs, and frozen vegetables. I like to serve at least two vegetables mixed at dinner time, like carrots and broccoli. The multi-colours add character to the plate.

Whenever I write a menu, I always include the Chef's Choice or Chef's Special throughout the rotation as it encourages using up the leftovers and creativity. There is no excuse for laziness in this area when you have a well-stocked pantry and freezer at your disposal.

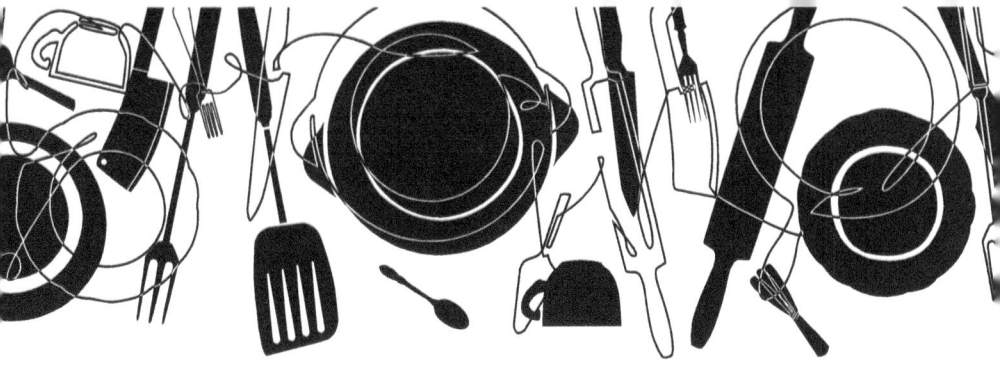

Chapter 20

It's time for some more funny business. I worked with another Chef at the retirement home. I loved her. She did not mince words and had no problem telling you exactly what she thought. She was so blunt and brutally honest that the shock factor of what she said was hilarious.

The first time I met her, I was hesitant because the general manager warned me about her blunt personality. I walked into the kitchen and found a shorter lady working and smiling while she prepared the meal. She looked up and saw me when I entered the door.

"Hello," She said politely. "I'm Tammy."

"Rick," I replied and smiled at her. "Nice to meet you."

"I swear and use inappropriate language. Do you offend easily?" She asked.

"Fuck no," I replied. We both laughed.

"Good. Because if you don't like it, you can kiss my fat fucking ass," Tammy said, laughing. I laughed my ass off too. Tammy is awesome.

"You are in retirement. The residents bitch about everything. Smile, and don't take it personally. Think of your worse customer. Now add forty of them. That is what you can expect. The meat, even though it crumbles to the touch, is always tough no matter what. You can whip the fucking hell out of your potatoes, but they will always say they are lumpy. You can have the soup and gravy boiling, and it's always cold. Welcome to hell," said Tammy with a massive smile on her face.

"Some of the servers are clueless, so you have to break down the terminology like you would for a kid. Keep it under two syllables. The one on days, keep it to one syllable if you can," Tammy continued and laughed.

"You are going to see all kinds of things. Don't get frustrated. You can't fix cranky and miserable. Some are away from their families and don't get visitors. They are not happy, so they take it out on the food. Try and do what you can. Like in the restaurant business, some will never be happy no matter what you do for them. Try your best and do what you can. Just understand this is the end of the road for them."

"Got it," I replied. "Don't take it personally."

"You got it," she confirmed. She laughed.

The server came in. She was a tall, blonde, slender girl. She smiled at Tammy.

"This is Kelly. She is the server on days. She is also an idiot, isn't that right, Kelly?" Tammy said, laughing.

"Tammy is a foul mouth bitch," shot back Kelly.

"Yup, and you can kiss my fat fucking ass," said Tammy laughing even harder.

"We have a love/ hate relationship," explained Kelly.

"Yeah, we love to hate each other," piped up Tammy. She laughed. It was like watching an old married couple who enjoyed insulting each other. Hilarious.

"Tammy, why don't you like me?" asked Kelly sincerely.

"Well, Kelly, it's because you are a stupid ass," replied Tammy. They both laughed.

"You are a fat ass, bitch," shot back Kelly. They continued to laugh.

"You can kiss my fat fucking ass," shot back Tammy. They were laughing even harder now. Wow. I am crass and crude. I could work here. These ladies are hilarious. Nothing offends them. Perfect.

I would have stayed if the pay was higher, but I love doing what I do now. I am a sous chef, and the same rules apply.

1. Swearing is ok but can not be directed at anyone as it becomes a personal attack. Dropping something, burning yourself, or a form of self-expression is ok.
2. Avoid Slurs. Hate speech is not acceptable. They are not funny and are just plain hate. Not cool.
3. Have fun and be respectful of each other's boundaries. Jokes are ok but watch the limits.

We had a resident who was Italian and swore at everyone in Italian. She refused to eat anything. Out of desperation, I made pasta Bolognaise or, in translation, pasta with meat sauce. It was taken out to her with garlic bread and cheese. One of the PSWs was Italian, and she offered to take it to her.

"It's pasta vaffanculo." Said the PSW presenting my pasta dish to her. The transalation to vaffanculo is 'go fuck yourself.' The resident started laughing.

"Yeah. Pasta Vaffanculo," she said, laughing. "Pasta Vaffanculo," she continued laughing to herself. She ate it all and wanted more. It became a thing. It was hilarious. From then on, when we ad a pasta dish, it was Pasta Vaffanculo. It still makes me laugh. It's my specialty. She ordered it by that name. Too funny.

Other specialties in Italian cuisine include Pompinara (Cocksucker) and cazzo (Cock), and Figa (Pussy). You can put those with anything. Fuck it. Have fun. Swear in other languages. It gets to be very funny.

* * *

Kelly got under my skin badly a few times. She was the only server on the day shift and liked to relay the resident complaints to me.

"They don't like the soup. The residents said it needs flavour." She announced in the kitchen. It was her favourite thing to say. It needs flavour.

"It's Campbell's," I informed her.

"I don't care. I am just relaying what the residents said. It needs flavour," she persisted.

"Are you kidding me? It's fucking Campbell's!" I told her again, even louder.

"Well, it's up to you to fix it," she shot back. Now I am pissed.

"Are you seriously this fucking clueless?!" I shouted at her. "It's fucking Campbell's Soup!! Call the 1-800 number on the package and bitch at them. I don't give a flying fuck about your complaint. I didn't make it, and it is NOT up to me to fix Campbell's fucking soup. You constantly tell me things need flavour and clearly show you have no fucking clue what you are talking about, do you? I don't want to hear another fucking word about the goddamned soup! Is that clear?! Know when to open your mouth on valid issues. This is not one of them. Now fuck off!" I screamed at her.

There are limits. I don't particularly appreciate getting like that, and I apologized to her for losing my mind. I reiterated to screen the issues. Also, she needs to know when to quit batting the beehive. When I say it is brought in from an outside company, that should be the end of it—persisting with something like that, and you are barking up the wrong tree.

* * *

With this home, I got to do a Chili Festival, and I went traditional. I love authentic food. I'm sure you have figured that out by now. I love the roots, the origin and the story behind it. I lose my mind when I go into a Greek restaurant serving Moussaka with fucking beef. I will walk out. It is made with lamb. I will accept a beef and lamb mix. That is acceptable. I get keeping the cost down but don't cheap out your heritage.

Traditional chilli is made with beef, chilis, seasonings. Kidney beans are optional. Chili Con Carne. The translation is Chilies with Meat.

CHILI CON CARNE

2 lbs Ground Beef medium of lean
1 Spanish onion diced
1 medium green pepper diced
1 ½ tsp Garlic
Salt to taste
Pepper to taste
2 tbsp Chili Pepper
28 -30 oz Diced Tomatoes drained
1 tsp Cumin
½ tsp Cayenne Pepper
1 cup Beef Stock
12 – 16 oz Kidney Beans (Optional)

1. Brown beef in a pan, drain and set aside.
2. Saute onions and peppers
3. Add Beef and remaining ingredients
4. Simmer for at least an hour, stirring occasionally.
5. For more heat, add another tbsp of chilli powder.

There is no mention of mushrooms, beans with pork and other ingredients that do not belong in chilli. Texas Red is even simpler. It contains beef, onions, seasonings and beef broth. I am a huge fan of Chili Con Carne with a Mexican cheese blend on top and toast or some cornbread.

At this event, it was for the fire department and the burn unit. I love to support these types of events. Anyway, I never understood the concept of adding so much heat to a dish to the point where it becomes inedible. Adding excessive amounts of spice does not make it better. Adding ghost peppers or Carolina reapers does not enhance the flavour. The idea behind chilli is not to have the most Scoville units.

For judging, you want it to be appetizing, smell good, have excellent meat to sauce ratio, great taste and then the aftertaste of the chillies. It should look, smell and taste good. Typically it should be red to brown.

At my event, there were a few entries where I wondered what they were thinking. There was one entry where the sauce was yellow. It looked like baby vomit. It did not taste good at all. It left an aluminum taste on my tongue. The favours did not blend well at all. I found it was most reminiscent of a bad experience with a type of liquor that caused excessive vomiting due to high consumption volumes. The after-taste was just as pleasant.

There is always someone who thinks the more heat, the better, and I have to tell you that at that point, you are wasting food by making it inedible. After one spoon of Satan's Soul Scorching Sauce, people are done with it. They don't want more. You burned our mouths out with this abomination to food. It's not enjoyable. It is going in the garbage where it belongs after the first spoonful. I have done enough where there was no prize for the hottest chilli. The attendees vote on it. You will find the average person is not looking for 2 Million Scoville Unit chilli. People love to eat, and it has to be palatable.

I won for the traditional taste and nearly sold out, whereas word will get out about your psychotic heat, and you can take the whole pot home and enjoy it by yourself. You can always wait until your friends are plastered and dare them to eat it. Whatever turns your crank.

However, I enjoy a good vegetarian chilli, and the same rules apply as previously stated. There must be flavour and a good solid to sauce ratio and an aftertaste that does not push psychotic boundaries.

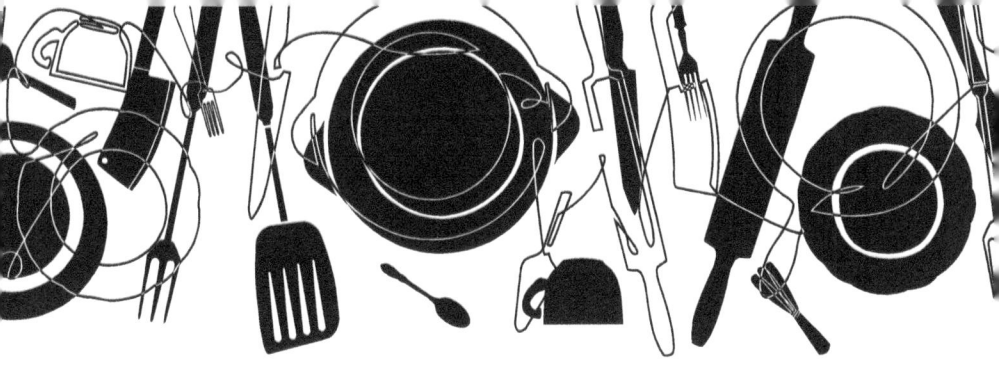

Chapter 21

I branched out to do my own thing. I opened a sandwich shop with fresh cut meats, hand-packed burgers and slow-roasted meats. We did it all in the store at a local market. Our Philly was terrific. I roasted the beef nice and slow for hours. It was sliced in-store, and we did half-pound beef with peppers and onions all bought at the market.

We had a Cuban, beef and cheddar, ham and Swiss, hotdogs, fresh-cut fries and poutine. The menu was simple, but it was good. There is nothing worse in markets than when you have other vendors that must do what you do. Beside me, the fish guy bought countertop deep fryers from the department store and sold fries.

The butcher would get his barbecue out and set it up outside and start selling hotdogs too. No wonder they are at the market. True bottom feeders. I should have known better as it was not the busiest market and later found out how poorly managed it was. I eventually pulled out of the market and sold the equipment. You can't run a shop when the others are constantly in your business and snooping on what you do so they can copy it in the same building. It also shows the level of success they have when they impersonate what you do. In short, they suck.

I got the opportunity to join up on a food truck and not team up with anyone in hindsight. Someone always gets the raw deal. One will always take advantage. In this case, I did. Some can talk a good game but fail to deliver. It was a husband and wife team. She is a PSW but passes herself off as a Chef. Her husband Dan was a chef; Stacey was not.

I did a few events with them, and always a story. We did an event where it was a food truck rally. Stacey's contribution was summer rolls she bought at the grocery store with a sauce out of the bottle, which pretty much sums up her talent level. The talent was cutting them in half and pouring sauce. They brought vegan items because they think it is a big thing. It is not.

Meanwhile, my sales carried the events with meat and French fries, but you know how it goes. Ther bills have to be paid.

They hustled their money by getting sponsorships from other businesses and, of course, nothing in return. They pass themselves off as high-end catering. The only thing high-end is the price.

Catering to special diets is a losing battle and not worth the price you pay. When you target the demographic with fad diets and specialty diets, you severely limit your sales potential. We did an event at a more significant food truck rally where it was Mac N Cheese-based.

"Are you interested in doing the mac N Cheese festival?" asked Dan.

"Sounds like fun. We could use a good event," I replied.

"It's also a competition, and the first prize is $5,000. The second prize is $2500, and the third is $1,000. I know we can win it," he said, trying to convince me.

"Okay, what is the entry fee for the event?" I asked.

"$2500, and attendance is usually around 100,000 persons," he replied.

"That sounds pretty good. If we do it right, it should be a moneymaker," I added.

"Are you in?" he asked.

"Yes, let's book it," I said with enthusiasm.

* * *

A couple of days later, I got a text. "We need another $2,000 for the city fee for business licensing. Sorry, bro. We got blindsided too."

I called the organizer. He informed me as long as we have our trailer inspected and up to code. There are no other fees. As for the event itself, everything was included in the registration fee. I even called the city hall where the event was taking place. Yes, they have a registration fee of $2,000 per year, but that is for brick and mortar stores in that city. Events are required to get their permits for the exhibitors as a special event permit. An event is a registered event, and the organizer has paid their fees and insurance; it is up to the organizer to collect their payments. Nowhere on the event registration were there any other fees except applicable sales tax. It would be very shady to add an extra $2,000 cost to the event.

I texted back. "I contacted the city, and no extra fees are required. I contacted the organizer, and all fees are included in the cost."

"Okay, I misunderstood something." I left this alone, but it should have been a warning sign. The only way he would have known about the city fees is by visiting that city's website. Conniving. He certainly made that sound convincing. It is time to err on the side of caution.

We had conversations about staff for the event. I was bringing one. They were getting a couple. We started strategizing for the event.

"What are we going to do?" asked Stacey

"Let's do pulled pork mac and cheese," I suggested.

"Beer and Bacon," suggested Dan.

"Is there a twist?" I asked.

"Listen to Dan; he knows his stuff," interjected Stacey.

"Oh, and I don't?" I asked. I am getting pissed now.

"Yeah, but we want to win," replied Stacey.

"Seriously?!" I shot back. Now I am pissed. A PSW is going to question me? Hell no. You are not a chef. You are a personal support worker, and your job is to bathe and help people use the toilet.

"Well, we have more invested in the trailer than you," said Stacey condescendingly and with just the right touch of Holier than thou. Bitch.

"Yeah, and you bring premade resale items you got at the grocery store and try to pass it off as your own like your summer rolls, for example. You got them straight from the deli and poured a sauce. My stuff sells. I make it; you don't," I shot back. Don't talk down to me bitch.

"Really?!" she shot back, challenging me.

"Yeah. $15 for two summer rolls you cut in half with 2 ounces of sauce. You picked up a knife and cut it. You broke a sweat. Amazing. Pure talent."I shot back.

"Okay, you two, enough," interrupted Dan trying to keep the peace. "We need to focus. We all have a lot of bills to pay and an event to plan for and hopefully win. If not, at least make some good sales," he added.

"Agreed." I shot Stacie a look.

"Ok. Pulled pork is going to be too costly. Let's use a beer and three cheese mac and cheese with bacon. Top it off with ranch dressing and green onions. I think that will work." Said Dan with confidence. I wasn't so sure. Pulled pork is always a winner.

"Okay, where are we getting the supplies? I have an account with a food packaging company. I will get the paper products and supplies." I offered. I also knew I could return what I don't use on a 30-day credit. It lessens my risk. My food carried the other events. Not theirs.

"We will get the food. We have an account to use for that," added Stacey.

"Ok. Let's get the recipe together," I suggested.

"I already have it," said Dan with confidence.

"Great, let's get the order in. How many servings?" I asked.

"The organizer said 15,000," replied Dan.

"Holy shit," I replied. This was huge.

We ended the Dan and Stacey show, and I went home. Yup, all about them. This event should be interesting and should tell a few things about the talent level.

* * *

There was a commercial kitchen in the market for rent, and it required cleaning—lots of it. The last time it was used, it was not cleaned afterwards and got neglected. There was caked-on guck all over the cast iron covers on the range. The charbroiler had burnt and caked on crud all over it as well. The range had slop dried and stuck to the front. It had not been cleaned in months, by the look of it. The floor was a cry in shame. The area doubled as a dumping ground for random shit like boxes, storage containers, unused equipment, and we had to clear a path to it.

It took us about 3 hours to get it cleaned up enough to use it. We had 3 of us working on it. It's unfortunate and quite disgusting to let a kitchen get neglected in that state. Shameful. I would be embarrassed to rent that out. Clean it for fuck sales. Make it appealing.

The Mac and Cheese Recipe

A beer, I believe it was a lager from a local microbrewery. I would use an IPA as long as it was not too hoppy or a stout beer.

Knorr Cream Base (add to hot water to make a lactose free, vegan-friendly, gluten-free cream)

Mozerella

Cheddar

Swiss Cheese

Scooby-Doo or Cavatapi noodles (Scooby-doo are probably one of the worse choices you can make for this application as they break very easily when cooked. They overcooked it. So mush is the result. You have to cook pasta just under El Dente in this application.)

Add ranch dressing and sliced green onions for garnish.

Mac and Cheese. Macaroni and Cheese. Macaroni noodles. There is a reason for it—short noodles. Penne, ziti, fusilli, elbows are perfect; Cavatapi is not. I was not happy with this choice at all. It was the Dan and Stacey show. I get to help pay for it. Oh boy. I just had no idea how much.

We made the sauce and put it in 4-gallon pails. It went in the spare refrigerator at the market. The market had a few of these refrigerators sitting idle. More than 23 pails were filled with the sauce. 92 gallons. 11, 776 oz. 2,944 - 4 oz servings.

I ordered 15,000 disposable serving containers, forks, 45,000 napkins for the event with the option to return them as long as they were not opened. I was going to police this. Something was telling me this is not going to turn out well. Listen to that voice.

* * *

The event was in a park in the downtown core, close to the highest population density of the city. There were condos and highrises all around us. A stadium across the street and an arena three blocks away with sporting events booked all weekend. There was no excuse for the lack of patrons: banners, street promoters, and loudspeaker promotions for the event.

We were set up on the side in an L cove for the initial setup just off the path. Another vendor showed up, and apparently, the spot we were assigned took a portion of her layout. She was not happy about this.

"Excuse me. Your trailer is on my spot. I paid for four 10 x 10 spots," she stated.

"You have tents. You can move easier than we can," replied Dan.

"the hell you are going to talk to me like that. You can move this trailer the hell out of here, buddy. I have been doing this event for ten years. I know the organizer. This is your first time, and you are off to a bad start," she shot back, and she was not having his shit.

'Is there a problem here?" asked security as they were driving the golf cart by and caught the end of it.

"Yeah, you can get this trailer and these people the hell out of here. They set up in my space and then give me attitude. Hell no. They can move and now," she affirmed.

"We are not moving until we are told to move. This is where we were told to set up," answered Dan sharply. He was not helping the situation.

"May I?" I asked, entering the situation. It had to be resolved. Dan was only escalating it.

"Go ahead," answered the lady whose spot we were encroaching.

"What if we moved the trailer back a few feet to let the tent in for set up. Would that help? We seem to have a little communication breakdown here." I asked.

"It would, but now I don't want you here because of him (pointing to Dan). That moment has passed once he started disrespecting me. You can all fuck of. Not you (pointing to me). You are trying to help, but it's a little too late." She said with disgust.

Ultimately we moved to the other end of the park and were set on the trail. After setting up the event again, Dan and Stacey decided it was not good enough yet again, and we moved. It went back off the trail. It was a shitty location.

Before we began, they wanted to lead us in prayer. Unbelievable.

"Dan, can you lead us in prayer?" asked Stacey.

"Really?" I asked.

"Yes, he's a good prayer. God listens to him," she replied, smiling. I rolled my eyes loudly.

"Heavenly Father, we ask for your divine guidance and direction to get through this weekend. We have put a lot forth and our faith in you to get us through. We ask you to help us make enough to turn a profit to continue to do your work. In Jesus' name, amen." Prayed Dan. A few subtle amens around the trailer. I rolled my eyes even louder. Pray for money. I thought that was taboo.

Another surprise was they got Vegan Mac N cheese. One of their friends made vegan mac n cheese in their house and paid over $600 for it. I tried a bit, and it was disgusting. It tasted like paper. The sauce has an aftertaste I could only describe as a medicine aftertaste. Chew an allergy tablet; it will be close to the shit taste in your mouth this garbage left behind.

"Vegan is popular. We wanted to corner the market on those sales," insisted Stacey.

"Yeah, nothing brings out the vegans like macaroni and cheese," I said sarcastically. "Yup, cream and cheese. Everything a vegan needs," I added with more dripping sarcasm.

"Have you tried it? It's pretty good," she insisted, trying to defend the wrong decision.

"Yes, I have, and construction paper comes to mind when I tried it. The sauce is disgusting and watery. It has an aftertaste like when you chew an aspirin," I said. I could not hold back. It was fucking disgusting.

"That's your opinion," she replied.

"Yes, and will be everyone else's too once they try that shit. Word will get out, and you are going to be stuck with it," I shot back.

"Vegan is popular, and it will sell," she said, trying to convince me. It is not working. The shit is disgusting. Case closed.

"You won't be able to give that shit away. You'll see," I affirmed.

In my opinion, if you want my vegan, Keto, Atkins menu-it's in the parking lot. Do you go to a mac n cheese event and want vegan? It's expensive and not a popular seller. In short, it's a waste of time, money and effort to make. It's looking for pennies and skipping the dollars. It loses money. The facts speak for themselves. These clowns held a group prayer at the food truck. We are losing money. Yup, God doesn't like you either. The power of prayer.

People walked past us, and the action was where we were the first time. I walked by, and the lady smiled and waved at me. Rub it in. They brought seven helpers at $500 apiece for the weekend, and I got 1. You know how this was going to work out—$ 4,000 in Labour charges.

I took $40 out of the pot for my incidentals. We walked to our hotel. They had to drive, and of course, they stayed at the Hilton because they have to have the most expensive of everything.

The next day yet another shit show off the beaten path. Slow sales while their staff stand around, walk around the venue and collect cash.

"Hey, I need to tell you something," said one of their employees.

"What's up?" I asked.

"Stacey's credit card didn't work last night, so they took the sales money and paid for all of the hotel rooms. We were stuck in the lobby for three hours waiting. It was a shit show," she informed me. That is 4 Hilton hotel rooms! It came out of sales! I am furious.

I went to the organizer to see what we could do to get traffic. He gave me flyers. I sent the useless staff they brought to give them out.

Make themselves useful. The games were getting out. Get the fans at the nearest gates to the even.

We had an influx but not much of one. Sluggish sales again for the second day. At least the organizer had the decency to move a ticket booth near us. It didn't help much. The buzz was the best-tasting mac n cheese. They told us we were in the running. I am sure they told everyone that.

Of course, I went up to Stacey sitting on her ass at the table outside—collecting the money. She is all about the money. The ten was covering up my logos as usual. It's all about her. Her Instagram is just like that too. All about her and her Chef facade.

"How was your stay last night?" I asked.

"It was okay, but my credit card didn't work, so I had to use the sales money…."

"Of course you did, and you made me pay for that too, didn't you? More money I get to payout. Excessive staff and now their rooms too. Did you buy them meals too? Jesus Christ, Do you think I'm made of money?! I have not taken a dime for my room, and you take it all for yours. That's fucking bullshit!!" I let her have it.

"Well, we paid for the food…."

"That does not make you entitled to every dime!! I paid half the rent for this event, and you take everything. Are you fucking kidding me?!" Stacey is a greedy, conniving bitch.

"Well, if we win, we are taking it all." She said with a smirk.

"Try it. Over my dead body and if you do. You are a greedy fucking bitch. You hind behind Jesus and pretend to be so good. You're not. Just another lying, greedy fucking bitch. Yeah, and you prayed for money too. What a joke. How's that working out? We are losing our ass, and you take everything! The power of prayer. Either God hates you too, or there isn't one, is there? You think I am pissed off now, you wait, and you will see what I am capable of…." I warned her.

"Your lack of faith in God is disturbing." She started to preach. I rolled my eyes again. "That right there is the problem, you are supposed to give 10 % of your earnings to Him, and you will be rewarded." She continued.

"10 % is all of the profits in food and beverage. Give your head a shake, and the way you are going, there will be nothing left but debt. I'm not paying it." I shot back. I could not believe we were having this conversation. Talk about delusional.

It was the last day of the event, and it was time to announce the winners and runner-ups. We didn't even place. I wasn't shocked. I was pissed right off. The winner was pulled pork mac n cheese. Is there an echo in the room/ Can I say I told you so?

Only seven vegan dishes got sold at $5 each. In short, a $565 loss on that product. Great contribution. They were happy with the sales on it. Catering to such a small percentage of the market, you will lose every time. If you want vegan mac n cheese at an event like this- it's in the parking lot.

Oh wait, it gets better. The tally for the weekend was enough to pay the overabundance of employees and fuel for the ride home. The conversation was like this:

"We didn't make enough of a profit," Stacey stated.

"You don't say..." I snarked back.

"Enough of that. We have a problem," Stacey continued.

"Yeah, you took the money to pay for the rooms at the most expensive hotel for you and your staff. You brought an excessive team at $500 each. Then there's the vegan mac n cheese—$ 600 spent for $35 in sales," I continued. "I want to be bought out of this sinking ship. I get to pay for your excessive staff's wages, their hotel rooms, and then I get to pay some more because of your gross mismanagement, don't I? You even sold some of the paper products, and I don't get shit from that either. Well, guess what, I'm not paying anything else," I was furious and disgusted.

"Well, we still have the problem t hand. There is not enough to pay everyone. Our sous chef gets $800; everyone else earns $500 except one of our employee's daughters. She gets $200, but I was hoping you could break it to them. I can't have my friend mad at me," she asked.

"Wow. Really? Fine. I don't care what they think, and if I had my way, they wouldn't be here anyway. I get to do your dirty work now because you don't have the backbone to do it yourself." I replied. I was in total disgust. I was pissed.

"Don't worry. Dan is trying to get investors at the event." She reassured me. The reality is they try to hustle 'sponsors' wherever they go. You can see the reward there already. You get absolutely nothing. It's advertising on a small one-foot square decal at knee level. Of course, I never got any of that either.

I went and broke the news to the staff and paid them. I wanted to skim the top and deduct $100 from each team member to cover my costs. There was fuck all left. Yeah, the power of prayer.

"Stacey put you up to it, didn't she?" asked her friend over the payment of her daughter.

"Of course, she doesn't have the guts to do it herself. So I don't have to tell you this is not my doing. I lost a lot of money this weekend, but at least you get paid. You should have gone home when you saw the shit show. Now I have to borrow money to drive my truck home. This is over." I replied.

I returned the unused packaging, and it was not out that much, thankfully. However, lesson learned. If they talk smooth-run away and do it yourself and always have a shareholders agreement.

* * *

I put mac n cheese on my menu, and Stacey had no problem commenting on my Instagram: "Dan makes the best mac n cheese there is."

So I replied: "Yup, it is so awesome it didn't even place at a mac n cheese competition,"

They kept putting the trailer in the parking lot at the market and, of course, not sharing a dime. With the toxic culture in the market, I ripped my equipment out and sold it. I will do another venture again, but not with anyone else. Stay away from charlatans.

They kept the mac n cheese sauce in buckets and tried to keep using it three months later—nothing like top-quality freshness there. The fridge with the sauce had a compressor failure, and the stock of sauce was lost. These two did not pay a dime of rent for the refrigerator either. Of course, I got blamed for it. They pass themselves off as gourmet when it is substandard food at best. Lesson learned. Always do things for yourself only. They are so full of shit they make me sick.

They call it an investment, but there is never a payout. It's worse than a Ponzi scheme. At least some got paid by Ponzi.

They posted a video of giving money to struggling businesses during the pandemic to make themselves look good. Some people will do anything for attention. They probably hustled that money too. Sickening. They should be called Copy Cat Catering because they have to do what everyone else is doing.

Since they like to copycat everyone else, their fry seasoning is Lawry's seasoning salt and garlic powder. They add Sprite or 7-up to their fish batter. Beer tastes better, but on a budget, it can work. It's not even theirs either; they stole that from another chef.

I made Cuban sandwiches with pork butt or shoulder with a southern seasoning mix. The seasonings were chilli powder, salt, black pepper, brown sugar, garlic, cajun, cumin (use a less as it is very earthy), paprika, onion powder, a small dash of Cayan pepper.

I laid it in a bed of mirepoix fat side up and added apple and pineapple juice to the water for braising liquid. I covered it and let it go low and slow. Take the cover off in the last hour and let it crisp up a bit at 350 F.

Let it rest, and then slice it nice and thin. I added ham and Swiss cheese on a nice hoagie-style roll, and I used a Dijon mustard instead of the cheap, vile prepared mustard. You will thank me. Dijon brings out a better flavour than prepared mustard by far. Use an authentic Swiss cheese slice, don't cheap out with processed Swiss-like cheese.

My Beef got braised as well. I liked to add leftover coffee in the braising liquid with a nice rub of salt, pepper, garlic, onion powder, a little cumin, basil, thyme, rosemary and a touch of oregano. This beef makes a melt in your mouth Philly as well.

The coffee in the braising liquid makes a lovely rich gravy. Add a bit of instant beef stock, and it brings out the flavour. Use that gravy for poutine with real cheese curds and fresh-cut fries; you will not be disappointed.

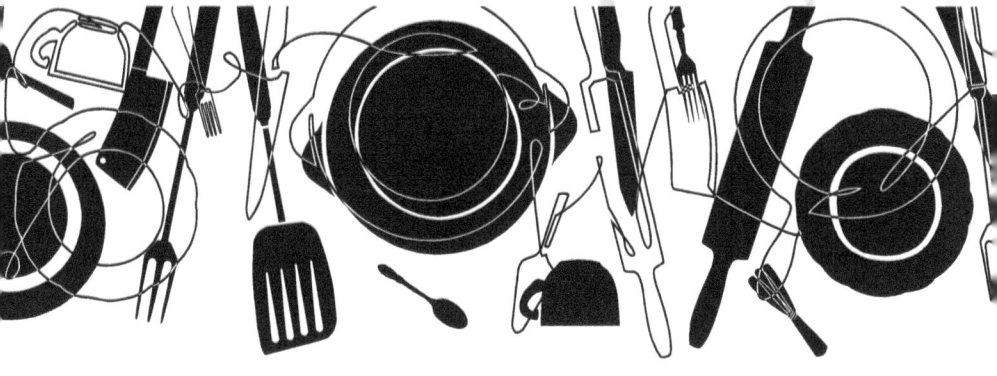

Chapter 22

Have you ever had a boss you can't stand? Have you ever left an employer because your boss sucked and you could not take any more of their shit? I have had to do that twice. It is not a good feeling. According to research, more than 75% of people quit their jobs because their boss influences them. I found this article at Business Insider.

Weak and inefficient managers can be the worse thing. They do not respect your time. Dismiss your feedback or suggestions, and refuse to listen to it. They don't trust anyone and hide when problems arise or shrug them off or pass the buck. The worse thing a boss can do is take credit for your work, according to research. They sweep things under the carpet, and their communication is one way. Their way. Poor listening skills.

Have you ever wondered why people hate their jobs and quit? More than half of us feel disconnected, have bad managers or the environment.

A few signs of a weak manager are they are not qualified or absent. I have had a few inexperienced managers. My least favourite was the maid of honour. Teresa was the head manager of the Shoreline retirement home. She hired her maid of honour to help her. She had her head so far up her friend's ass, and she was placed second in command. The lack of experience was painfully obvious. She dismissed everything I had to say even though I have more than 20 years of experience in the field and have even done banquets of 1000 or more.

For a party of 180 guests, she bought one 15 pound turkey and one beef. She was so rude that she even brought in her mother, who is supposed to be a chef. By these standards, she is a fucking line cook, no more. Any chef with half a brain would know you need at least 6 or 7 turkeys to feed a crowd of that size.

She refused to listen to anyone other than her mommy, dearest. The event was a total shit show and a miserable failure. He stuck up bitch of a mother was on beef and did minimal work but stand there and pretend to be the queen bee of my kitchen. Standing over the beef while her oblivious twit daughter was barking orders at the staff to try and make this a success. I was furious.

I decided to let her go down hard and put myself on garnish and mashed potatoes. Erikunt knows everything. Erika. I despise this bitch. There is nothing worse than having an oblivious twit running a show. It is doomed for failure before you even get started. After meeting her clueless mother, it is safe to say the apple does not fall from the tree.

She is a great chef. She helps her dumb-ass, talentless hack daughter with one magical turkey. Perhaps they were expecting Christ to show up and feed the masses. We ran out of meat before everyone made it through the buffet line.

"Oh my god, we are going to run out of meat," she exclaimed when she ran back into the kitchen.

"Wow. There's a shock. Who didn't see that coming? Oh, and you are a Chef. I can see you are very talented since you are a part of this train wreck," I answered in a sarcastic and condescending tone. I looked right at her and her line cook bitch mother. She does nothing at her job other than cooking the food. I would assume out of a packet or box.

"You are not helping." She replied.

"I offered when you only ordered one, but you would not listen because "You Know It All." Do you want toothpicks so we can have turkey tapas? Even that ship has sailed, you ran out. Your experience is showing." I shot back. Her mother glared at me. Tough shit, 'Chef.' You are just as stupid, and it is painfully apparent.

"We will discuss this later," she replied. She was getting annoyed and trying to show authority, but I kept throwing logs on the fire. That is precisely what stupid people deserve. Rub their failure in their face.

"There is nothing to discuss. Enjoy your failure. There is no help for you. It would take a miracle to help you, and sadly, there is no such thing as miracles. I guess your party will have to go down in flames." I said and smiled at the clueless twit. I had no respect for Erika from the moment I met her.

She got so desperate she cranked the oven on high to cook two small turkey breasts from the freezer. They were Frozen rock solid. Inside I was dying of laughter. I even let out a chuckle. It was like the Hindenburg again. Oh, the humanity. She was getting upset I was not helping her. Seriously, what did she expect me to do? Perhaps wave a wand and make more cooked turkey appear? OH, I am so sorry dumbass, there is no helping you on this one.

I wish I were out in the hall watching the unhappy guests lose their minds. All my events worked. This event was a complete disaster. She wanted to impress her friend and show she could do it. She even ignored other managers who have experience. She is so confident and all-knowing. The know-it-all-know-nothing twit is in charge. I love it. Chefs are evil, and we will watch your ass sink when you want to be arrogant like this clueless twit.

I know other skilled tradespersons like this too. Since you know everything, mechanics, plumbers, electricians, and other experienced professionals will gladly do what you ask for a price. You are paying for it. I know some who love to have to go and fix your YouTube class repairs. You mess up whatever you touch and expect the professional to make it all the better for you. Oh, you should have taken our advice all along. Amazing.

Teresa came storming into the kitchen. She was furious. This complete and total disaster reflects on her and her leadership. This should get good. She knows her friend is a complete idiot. At least that would happen anywhere else. It would be termination of employment. This is not a mistake. It is a monumental fuck up. It is gross negligence.

"What the hell is going on in here?' she demanded. Of course, she was looking at me.

"This disaster is all her," I said, looking at Erika. I smiled at her and her useless twit mother.

"It's my first time," pleaded Erika.

"No, you ignored everything anyone said to you because you know it all. You even brought your mother because she is such a great Chef, and clearly, she isn't. You wanted this thing to be all about you, and now it is. I give you full credit. Just like you deserve,"

"That is not how you talk to a manager," stated Teresa.

"I don't care. The trainwreck is her show, and she gets all the credit." I replied.

"Well, it's her first one…" said Teresa.

"No. You came in here to blame someone, and it's your friend, so now it's okay," I replied. I am disgusted, but you can see how this is going to go. Erika can mess up everything she touches, but it's okay. If it were anyone else, Teresa would unleash the fury on them. Erika just stood there with a smug look on her face.

I know that look, the same of a spoiled brat kid that can do no wrong. Erika should have been walked out the door on the spot, but she was the maid of honour. Teresa is making excuses for her. More excuses would be coming for this dullard.

With the signs of a weak manager, it is obvious they both are. The entire debacle got swept under the carpet because Erika can do no wrong. It is far from the only issue from the witless wonders.

They wanted to throw me under the bus for the whole thing. I could have saved the event, but it would be unethical. How about a page from the first Chef I worked with and his dark humour. I get it. I had all the ingredients right there in the kitchen for Braised Bitch. Again, please don't take it seriously, but let's laugh anyway, no matter how tempting it is.

Erika's fat ass could have easily fed 50 people alone. Add her arms and thunder thighs, and could have got to about 100. Make some sweetbreads out of her hypothalamus and, of course, kidney pie. She liked her wine, so I am sure it is well marinaded from the inside out.

Add Tanya into the mix, and we would have some leftovers for stew for another day. Erika's daft twit mother, and now we have a feast.

It's like a pig roast, but we are making the world a better place all at the same time. Pigs are smart; these bitches aren't. They proved they are not and will do it again. It was their duty to feed the guests, and they re still hungry. The job must be completed, and as a chef, it is your job to make sure guests are satisfied. If you like them, you can always use the workplace snitch in the recipe below. They squeal like a little piggy anyway, so you might as well treat them like one. It improves morale, and everybody wins. Wow, this is psychotic. Never do this. Killing is wrong. In North America, you will be locked up for life. In other places, a death sentence. Get it out of your system, but it is best to move away from trash like this.

BRAISED BITCH OR SNITCH (DEPENDS ON THE MOOD. BOTH ARE DESPICABLE)

One stupid and useless person, the world would be better off without them around. For the love of God, please make sure they won't be missed. I recommend someone with less than 100 Facebook friends. (A total loser). This is dark humour not to be taken seriously. This is how I would prepare pork. A snitch is a swine in my books, so pork works.

20 pounds onions coarsely chopped
10 pounds carrots coarsely chopped
10 pounds celery coarsely chopped.
Red wine.
Pineapple Juice
Apple Juice

Bitch Rub (salt, pepper, garlic, brown sugar, Cajun, chilli powder, paprika, onion powder, cumin, ginger.)

Method.

1. Preheat ovens to 350 F
2. Cut into easy-to-carry parts. A sharp knife through the joints helps. You don't need a hernia trying to lift them.
3. Line the bottom of each pan with mirepoix. (50% onions, 25% carrots, 25% celery)
4. Use bitch rub generously to cover all areas and place over the mirepoix.
5. Fill pans with water, a little pineapple and apple juice, and concentrated chicken stock until 2 inches deep. We need to pass this off as pork roast. My recommendation is Pork. They are swine and treat them accordingly.
6. Cover and braise in the oven until tender or internal temperature of 165 F. This should help it fall off the bone.
7. DO NOT CARVE IN FRONT OF GUESTS! You will be locked Up For life!!
8. Use liquids to make gravy. Make lots of sauce. Add red wine to finish the sauce.
9. Serve to as many guests as possible. You don't want too many leftovers. Offer leftovers to your guests. Don't keep mementos.
10. Heavily scrub kitchen when done. Use bleach in your cleaning solutions. Do not mix ammonia. It makes Chloramine Gas, and it can kill you, plus it will draw attention. We don't want that.
11. Realize that you will never be let out and spend the rest of your life behind the glass when you do get caught. No matter how careful you are, it will happen. Nobody is worth the jail time.

I added this recipe because waste not, want not. Losers do serve a purpose. If there is an apocalypse, we won't go hungry.

STEAK AND KIDNEY PIE

Two kidneys small dice
Red Wine
Leftover Braised Bitch or beef diced small
Premade Pie Shells
Salt to taste
Pepper to taste
Garlic to taste
Two 0z Butter
Two bottles of dark ale
4 oz flour
8 oz mushrooms sliced
Three onions

1. Sweat the vegetables in a pan with butter
2. Combine ingredients in a pan and simmer.
3. Pour into Pies shells
4. Bake at 350 F until golden brown.

We all say things, but it is best to remove yourself from the poisoned environment. I found a much better job, and they can be miserable and oblivious to their heart's content. The problem is that the industry has taken a turn for the worse, enabling the toxic behaviour of snitching, sabotaging, and ganging up on others.

Chapter 23

I love how favouritism works out. Putting an utterly oblivious dullard in charge of something they know nothing about in any way. Erika was in charge of the kitchen now at the home. It was apparent we did not like each other. We know how this is going to go. I had a target on my back for not taking the shit for her stupidity and mistakes, and quite honestly, I did not care.

I had an online side business and was making more than being in this poisoned shit hole. I did not want to be there anymore anyway. I was biding my time for the store I was opening. I needed change for a fun environment. The kitchen used to be like that, but then the dullards came. There are too many to count. I just had to wait it out. Then I get Erika. The most oblivious twit I ever met.

It was funny because Teresa could not say anything against me, she loved the food, and then this idiot maid of honour came along and now I'm the problem. Bulshit. It was time to give me a raise. That was the problem, plus Erika had a stick up her ass, and she had no reason to. She was oblivious and had no idea what to do in the kitchen. She had zero experience, and it showed in everything she did.

She observed and asked questions that showed her lack of knowledge, including food storage, why we braise the meat and even the basics. She walked around and made notes. We already hated each other.

Unfortunately, it was hard for me to answer her without letting on she was annoying me. Very hard.

The day cook was an issue that was never addressed. She had no experience and got the job because her friend used to work in the kitchen. She was to cook breakfast and made pizza for a living. I did that when I was 16. I am impressed—a 40 something-year-old working with teenagers. Kristy.

I had less than half an hour to fix her mistakes and mostly finish the tasks at hand. The salad was never done or sandwiches incomplete. There was always something that needed attention. The excessive smoke breaks may have had something to do with that. When I worked that shift, I was standing around when the other person came in. My service was ready t go ahead of time. The way the handover should go. It was like that at the other home too. Not here. There was an excuse for everything. There was even a schedule for tasks. This individual never followed it.

With the previous manager we had, I wrote the menu with her. My menu was inspired by their travels to the Gulf Coast and bus trips in their younger years. It had things that I hoped would inspire happy memories. I remembered what Tammy said, "It's the end of the road," and I wanted to make it somewhat more enjoyable. Meals do that. I also knew it was what they liked to bitch and complain about the most too.

I had a tough resident to please. She was next to impossible to please. The server could not communicate with her. It didn't help. The resident was rude too.

"You go talk to her," said the server.

I went out in the dining room and heard her say to another resident. "Oh, here we go."

"You came to talk to me? I don't want to talk to you. Make me a fucking cheese omelet. Do you have that? A Cheese Omelet. Now, go." She demanded.

I couldn't believe this bitch. I went back to the kitchen and made it. I put it up in the window. "Take this to Princess Peachka out there," I said.

"Ok, got it." She stopped. "Did you just say Peachka?" she laughed. "That is my language!" she was howling with laughter now, and so was I. "Yes! She is a peachka. A big peachka." We laughed more. She left and came back and was howling with laughter. Peachka is a European word for cunt. Bosnian. The name kind of stuck as per how rude she was. Of course, it was back of house only. There is always trash talk in the kitchen. Deal with it.

We had another resident who liked to make up stories like how he can only eat pasta and onions in mayo as per his doctor's orders. Bullshit. No doctor on Earth would suggest something like that. We had a resident who wanted her food pureed at a previous home because she didn't want to chew anymore. The shit doesn't stop.

* * *

Erika comes along and wants to change everything. The menu was not up to her standards, even though the residents loved it. She wanted more salads and high-end food. Yeah, good luck with that. High-end gourmet on a $7 budget. Her know-it-all-know-nothing attitude was coming out. I was not allowed to do the new menu. She hired another cook, and I will always regret giving a reference for this backstabber. Jen.

Erika would come into the kitchen to help. She managed to burn frozen pies and tried to blame the instructions on the box.

"I'm sorry I burned the pies but enter exhibit A," she said, handing me the box. "I baked it for 55 minutes on 350 F."

I read the box. I chuckled. "It's 325 F for 45-50 minutes on a convection oven. You followed the directions for a conventional oven," I replied and handed her back the box. It shows you what this two-bit Betty Crocker knows. Nothing. I thought we already established that too. Why not again?

"Oh. Does it make that much difference?" Erika asked. Now there is a stupid question—the evidence in your hand. Also, with the added nicely charred and blackened edge of your pies.

"It does. Enter exhibit B," I said, pointing to the charred pies.

"Well, you don't have to rub it in," she said, getting on the defence.

"Sorry. You asked." I replied. She left the kitchen. Good riddance.

* * *

Jen got tight with Erika and wrote the menu. It was pretentious, and everything had a garden salad. There were hardly any potatoes or rice. There was salad. Salad is not filling, and you are hungry later. I had issues where residents would come for a second meal because Jen and Erika tried to fill them up with fucking salad.

I would walk in at 11 and have to fix Kristy's shit or help her finish constantly. I was getting sick of this place. Jen, who I once considered a friend had her ass so far up Erika's ass it was disgusting. She kissed it constantly, and the menu was from the same banquet place I worked. There was no originality whatsoever.

Then the writeups began. I got a written because I am rude, use foul language, and am condescending, intimidating, and insulting to the staff.

"Are you kidding me?" I asked Erika.

"Princess Peachka is insulting," she said

"Oh really, and that happened months before you got here. Let's address what it is. You burned the pies because you can't follow instructions on the box. You found how I answered your stupid question about the difference between a convection oven and a convection oven was insulting because I pointed out your inefficiency, and now I have to pay for it," I shot back.

"You throw things is another complaint I got,' she replied with a smirk on her face. I wanted to throw a punch right in her throat.

"Wow. Here's why: The pan I grabbed was hot. Did you want me to hold onto it, keep burning myself, and gently place it in the sink? Give your head a shake. You get misinformation and run with it. Pathetic! I don't remember you asking anything. You just run with a snitch report." I informed her. This stupid bitch is something else.

"You are rude and condescending," she added

"Oh, was I rude to you?" I asked in a snotty condescending tone. "Here, maybe you should make an effort to be smarter, and I'll be nicer.

You're rude. You brought your mother in and undermined me for the party. You're the stupid ass that bought one turkey to feed 180 people. Is that smart? No. It isn't. You burnt pies because you couldn't even follow written instructions. As for bad language, I have heard it out of everyone in this building, including you. Can you say, hypocrite?" I continued being condescending. Yeah, when I have to talk to someone that stupid. I will be condescending. I am surprised she could say the word condescending and even more surprised she could spell it. I will give credit to spell check. It's a big word, and it's bigger than her IQ. The big question is: Can she spell it? It's such a big word.

Here's another big word and probably how she got the job: Cunnilingus. She was referred to as the work wife by Teresa. Dumb as a stump, so she must be good at something. It's the only thing I can think of that makes any sense: Cunnilingus.

For those who do not know what Cunnilingus is: its simple meaning is "Muff Diving." We can have some fun now. Fur trading, carpet licking, polish the pearl, eating pussy, and a good old-fashioned pussy licker.

You are what you eat.

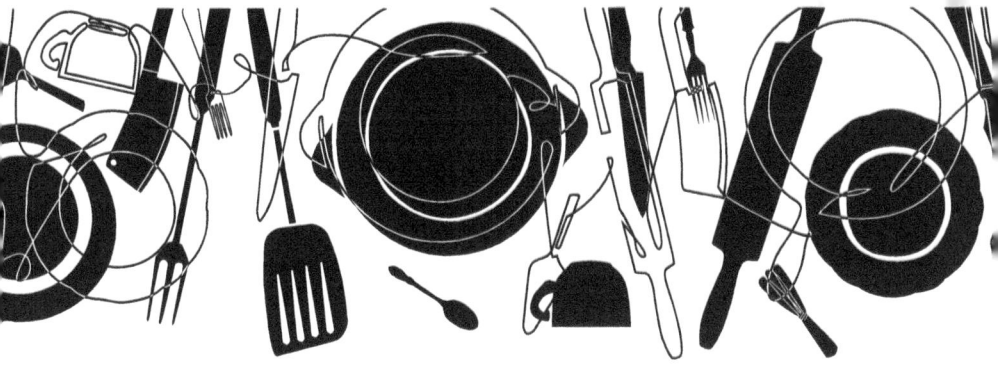

Chapter 24

Kristy was not fun to work with, and I loved it when it was her day off. Jen had it done on time. The amount of trash-talking behind each other's backs was appalling. Kristy hated my guts, and I did not care. She was nice to my face, but the shit she said behind my back was something else. It is the typical behaviour of the keyboard warrior. Talk all kinds of smack on social media and hide behind the computer.

She liked to run to Erika and Teresa about anything she could. She would leave the flat top a ness and leave it for me to clean. I refused. I don't use it, so I am not cleaning your mess. When she did clean it, she left her bucket of wastewater beside the flat top. She liked to leave her cardboard and garbage behind for everyone else to deal with it instead.

She left toast in the oven daily as she used it like a hot box. It was left on, and walk out the door without saying anything. Steam wells ran dry and were completely ignored. She looked for recognition when she finished on time. On a regular day, she relied on my help to get her out of the weeds daily. The gratitude was more snitching and lies.

For seniors, it is best to put the toast on the steam table for a bit of softness. Deliveries came at 9 AM and were still sitting on the floor outside the fridge at 11 AM when I started because she was always "too busy."

"Too busy" means talking shit about everyone else and countless smoke breaks. When you talk shit about your co-workers, one will always let the truth be told. I let it falter and let Teresa and Erika see what was going on. I didn't run and snitch. They saw it for themselves. It was my responsibility to clean up after her and fix her mistakes in time for service. I had half an hour, whereas she had six hours and still couldn't do it.

I got sick and tired of fixing soups made with 2-inch cuts of crudite or raw vegetables. It is not appetizing. I am sick of scraping the burnt off banana bread to try and serve it to the residents. I am sick of cleaning up her shit. I left the bucket of wastewater to see how long it would sit there. Two weeks went by, and the clueless twits finally asked me to take it out. I pointed out how long it sat there. Nothing was ever done about it. Kristy liked to snitch ad they like lying snitches.

She regularly left eggs boiling on the stove with no timer and walked out at service with no handover. The eggs were so overcooked they were green. All we needed was ham. We could serve green eggs and ham for everyone. Her egg salad contained so much dill that it was green continually. Am I supposed to fix that? Again green eggs and ham.

"Why so much dill?" I asked.

"I like dill," she responded.

It brought me back to the plate covered in chocolate sauce and sprinkles. Sprinkles for everyone! Dill for everyone!

"I need you two to work out an outing for team building," suggested Teresa.

"I have just the thing. You like to run your mouth behind my back and talk shit, so I suggest we go the range. I get the rifle, and you can hold the target over your face," I suggested sarcastically. However, there was some truth to it. "I promise I won't miss, and then it's your turn." I was wondering if she would catch on that she would be dead.

"You're funny," she shot back sarcastically.

"Just think of the fun we could have," I added sarcastically.

"You're an asshole," she remarked.

"Do you want to know what you are?" I asked.

"I already know what you think of me," she replied.

"Good. A talentless, lying, backstabbing trailer trash waste of skin. Did I leave anything out?" I shot back.

"That's enough, you two," said Teresa.

"Does anyone else want some honesty?" I asked. I was on a roll. "The head nurse's daughter complained. I said, "Fuck" but it is ok for her to tell everyone she got her pussy waxed at college in her esthetics class. It's ok for her to say "Fuck", "Bitch", "Cunt", "Asshole," and "Cocksucker" You have to love the double standards. No discipline for her. She can do no wrong."

"That's enough," reaffirmed Teresa. You guessed it, that issue was never to be addressed. You have to love double standards.

* * *

Jen was a double agent for Erika and me. It was for what served her best at the time. You know she favoured Erika. Erika gave her a shift to make her god-daughter cupcakes. Elmo cupcakes with company ingredients on company time. Anywhere else, that is a termination notice—theft company time and assets. Was Erika polishing Teresa's pearl? I will say yes. Since they both hate the word, I will say it. It must have made them MOIST. M-O-I-S-T.

She did not like Kristy either and loved to repeat whatever stupid thing Kristy said.

Kristy said this one to Jen, and it became a running joke:

"Sometimes I'm smarter than you, and sometimes you're smarter than me."

What a fucking idiot. Do you know how stupid you have to be to say something like that? A complete fucking idiot. We used it for mockery daily every time one of us made even a hint of a mistake. It deserves nothing but the finest ridicule.

* * *

Teresa liked to micromanage and stick her nose in where it didn't belong. She felt that shepherd's pie was too messy and wanted it to be cut like a cake. She expected me to get to stay all in one piece. It's cottage pie. Shepherds don't herd cattle. They herd sheep.

"I don't like how this looks a mess. I talked to a chef friend, and he said use egg whites to make it stay in one piece," she said, sticking her nose in where it doesn't belong. That is the problem with micromanagement. Knowing fuck all and making suggestions. Do you know how fucking dry that would be?

"It is a wet dish with loose beef, vegetables, mash potatoes and gravy, so I will not deviate from the traditional recipe, sorry," I affirmed. I don't care what Teresa thinks.

"Well, I want you to do it. I am the manager, not you," She said, throwing her authority around.

"Do you know how dry that is going to be?" I asked.

"Figure it out," she said. There was no chance in Hell I was doing this one. Back to the rules- your opinion is not in the recipe.

COTTAGE PIE
(SHEPHERD'S PIE AMERICANIZED)

Mashed potatoes
Butter
Onions sauteed
Diced carrots, peas, corn
Ground beef
Beef Broth
Salt and Pepper to taste.

1. Brown the beef and drain.
2. Saute the vegetables, but most use the frozen vegetables, so steam them until hot and soft.
3. Add the beef to the vegetables with broth. Simmer 10 minutes
4. Layer the meat on the bottom of the pan and cover it with the mashed potatoes.
5. Bake at 400 F until brown and bubbling.

Amazing. No egg whites or mention of serving it like cake. Make it up as you go, you lying fucking bitch. Then if I did like you asked, you would bitch it was dry. You would want it Moist. There's that word you hate, bitch-MOIST. You are so fucking stupid and full of shit. If you think this is the end of this shit, it isn't.

I got pulled in for a meeting. I got handed an improvement schedule on making better time management even though dinner was never late. How to improve my skills and assess myself on a personal level for ways to improve. FUCK YOU!!!

Now here is where the sickening part begins. Teresa and Erika both knew I was misdiagnosed with Bipolar 2, and after paying for two re-assessments out of pocket, it was deemed I am not. I was being weaned off the lamotrigine, which is an anti-psychotic that I did not need.

These two bitches were aware of it, and they started their shit at this phase. It speaks volumes about someone who has to play games and cause shit during this period. It was to try and set me off. Teresa is a nurse by trade. This behaviour is wholly planned and manipulative. It is a game to see if they can make me snap.

I even went to Teresa and told her what was going on to be proactive. Proof of weak, manipulative, conniving, vindictive and lying cunt that she is. It takes an exceptionally rotten person to pull off this shit while someone has a mental issue, especially when they asked her for some help. Teresa and Erika pull their bullshit now. When you are managers, you are the most despicable, unprofessional, the lowest type of pathetic piece of shit. I expect this shit from high school students. Let me spell it out: L-Y-I-N-G F-U-C-K-I-N-G C-U-N-T-S

Let's look at lamotrigine. It is an anti-epileptic medication and is also used for bipolar to delay episodes. Side effects can include mood and behaviour changes, depression, anxiety, agile, hostile, hyperactive, suicidal thoughts or self-harm. Source: www.Drugs.com

I refused to do it. Are you fucking kidding me? Some clueless people like these two stupid bitches should stick to what they are good at and leave everyone else alone. They got upset I couldn't make an outside round tender like Prime Rib even though it was braised for hours the day before. Putting lipstick on a pig like I had to do with Kristy's garbage food. Stick to Cunnilingus, bitches.

* * *

"We called this meeting because your time management and food quality have diminished," Erika started.

"Oh, has it now?" I shot back. "Yeah, and you couldn't even heat stew without burning in. Do you think your talentless ass can judge me? Not one meal has ever been late, and you want to talk about 'time management' This should be good." I scoffed.

"Your fried chicken breading went soft in the steam table…." Continued Erika.

"Are you seriously this stupid?! Meat contains moisture, and it breaks down the breading. Have you ever had fried chicken before, you stupid bitch?" I am pissed now.

"Your turkey was dry…" she continued

"You're a fucking liar!" I was screaming now.

"Your work is substandard," shot back Erika.

"You have no standards. Burnt frozen pies, one turkey to feed 180 people, burnt stew where you just had to heat it, Substandard. You learned a new word, and you use it for everything. Do you want to know what substandard is, bitch? Look in the mirror. You fuck up everything you touch. Do you expect me to fix Kristy's mistakes in under half an hour? It's putting lipstick on a pig." I responded. I was letting them have it. When liars make up shit, you get disciplined no matter what you say, so let them have it. Especially these lying cunts.

"There was nothing wrong with the turkey. However, the shepherd's pie is still a mess, and you refuse to clean it up like I asked," confirmed Teresa. "And since you refuse to complete the assessment as I asked, I will give you a one-day suspension for insubordination," she continued. Erika laughed.

"You want to laugh? How about we look at your menu and the empty freezer that used to be full of frozen vegetables. How about the bare fridge where we have tons of greens for salad. You think salad is cheaper than starch and a vegetable." I shot back. I threw a costing sheet at them to prove salad costs more than double a starch and a vegetable. "Explain this!"

"You're out of line!!" Screamed Tereasa.

"And you are clueless, and it shows," I shot back. "Eggwhites in shepherd's pie, and you can't fathom that breaded chicken breaks down when it sits. OBLIVIOUS!! You have to make shit up! Fucking liars!!" I shot back.

"He has no respect for you," said the union rep.

"Really? What was your first fucking clue? They are liars, stupid and have to make up shit ever since that stupid bitch started here. You just sit there and let them gang up and make up fucking lies." I shot back, pointing to Erika.

"You also operate on LIFO instead of FIFO," added Erika.

Kitchens operate by FIFI. First In First Out. Every chef knows that. We label and date things to prevent loss of product. Always use the oldest items to go out first. Erika is a pathetic liar and has no talent. She has to make shit up to cover her lack of skills and knowledge. LIFO stands for Last In First Out. She probably just learned the term and wanted to use it.

She learned 'substandard,' and I will bet she can't even spell it.

"We already established you are a bullshit liar, so why not add another one, liar. You are just stupid and should be seen and not heard," I shot back.

"Are you calling me a liar?" asked Erika, trying to be intimidating.

"Right to your fucking face!" I stormed out of the meeting. I took the one day and quickly took a temp position in a printing shop to get out.

It took all I had not to throw the recipe book in the deep fryer and watch it fry. I also talked myself out of emptying the fryer on the floor my last shift, where I walked off the job. I wanted to order a super sticky meme with a Monk sitting on the floor, "No I in Team But U in Cunt" and stick it to the fridge. I wanted it so sticky it would damage the wall when you peeled it off.

Here's another thing for this leader-shit team, they let a server work alone on the midnight shift on the Dementia Floor by herself as a PSW with no formal training whatsoever. Why? Because she came from the same country as Teresa, and she was the main snitch that lied through her teeth and was on her phone texting more than anyone else. Of course, she complained about everyone else covering her substandard work.

That is the perfect textbook toxic environment where management disciplines employees based on snitch reports. It is a toxic environment where they make up bullshit to nail staff that doesn't kiss their ass and conform to the contaminated environment. It is the environment where the snitch has reached total control and power and is enforced by weak and incompetent management. It is a bullying environment by the mean girls club.

Jen was part of that group too. We are no longer friends. I will kick her square in the jaw with steel-toed shoes if I see her begging on the street and spit in her face afterwards. I have no respect for a snitch and a liar.

Those stupid bitches wanted me to make their food too. Do you remember the rule about not fucking with someone who has access to your toothbrush or your food? I made their food 'special' for quite some time. Bon Appetite, Bitches.

I connected with the previous chef, and he went through something similar. They loved him until it was time to give him a raise. The same shit happened. A happy employee is a former employee of this place. Substandard? Gaslighter?

Gaslighting is psychological abuse where a person or group makes a person question their worth, sanity, perception of reality. They make the other person feel they are the problem and question themselves. They lie, deny and manipulate the other persons. It causes anxiety, depression.

The gaslighter does it for control of others due to their entitlement. Those who gaslight are narcissists who need constant attention, admiration, lack empathy and feel better than everyone else. In this case, she liked to spoil herself with $500 pairs of shoes. And pearl polishing session, I am sure.

When you are in that situation, it is best to get out. Take any job, temporary or whatever you can and leave. Like I said, former employees are happy employees—all of them.

I walked out, and it was a huge blessing. Where I am now, we get rave reviews, and I work with a competent team that supports each other. We also get it done and have fun. We are snitch-free—substandard, my ass.

As for Jen. I sent her a nice Facebook message on new year's eve. "I see you are no longer there. Ass kissing and snitching gets you nowhere. Happy New Year!"

Here's another part for you: once you burn a bridge with a chef, we will recommend you to anyone. I have no problem letting colleagues know about you. I know they will do it to me as well.

In Jen's case, I had no problem letting her know where she stood with me before I cut her off. She was kissing their asses so much that she thought she was in charge. Her menu sucked and showed a complete lack of knowledge of food costs. Salad does not fill anyone up and is a higher cost.

We had this conversation before I left. Jen didn't like I was adding starch to the dinner menu as I saw fit. Starch fills them up better than salad.

"You need to follow my menu and stop giving them potatoes and rice with it," said Jen.

"Let's get one thing clear. You will never be my boss. Write that down until it registers. As for the starch, I will continue to do so as I am tired of people coming back less than an hour later for seconds because you and your fucking salad don't fill them up. Great job." I affirmed. Trust me. I will not recommend her to anyone. I will not subject anyone to a snitch and a backstabber.

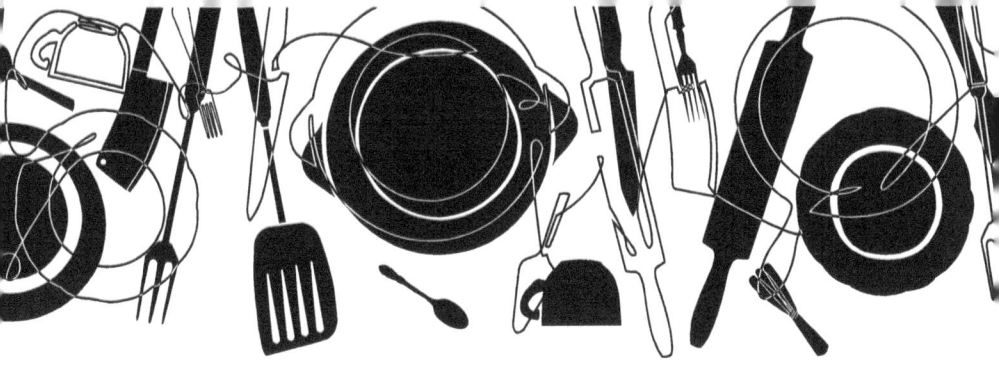

Chapter 25

In this industry, you have to shake your head at some of the intelligence levels people portray. In Erika's case, she was still at the level of the Little Engine That Could. It was probably the last book she read. The behaviour is juvenile and has no place in the workplace. It is even more sickening coming from management. What's even funnier is Erika couldn't handle the job when no one would cook for her stupid ass and had to resign and retrain for something else. Cunnilingus doesn't make you qualified for shit. Exit stage right, fuck off and die.

The thing that annoys us as chefs is a fundamental lack of courtesy and the followings list compiled through online searches, talking to other chefs, and my own experiences. There are several variations, but I have my list.

1. Guests who arrive just before close and want full service. We are ready to go home. Coming in later than half an hour before we close is just inconsiderate. The kitchen must be cleaned and shut down. I usually close the kitchen half an hour before close. In those cases, I will run the deep fryer items like wings, fries and other appetizers.
2. No Shows when a reservation is booked. We set that table aside for you and could have easily used it for someone else. Tables

are the source of revenue. You cost us revenue. A no-show is inconsiderate and rude.
3. Making up allergies like gluten-free and then eat a piece of cake or pie. Nobody likes a liar.
4. Guests who ask stupid questions. There are too many to list. "Do you work here?" I love that one. I had a co-worker who had an excellent response to it. "Nope. I have bad taste in clothes." I had one that was just made me shake my head. "Is the hamburger made with beef?" It is tough to respond to that when the menu clearly says "all beef" without trying not to be an ass. It is challenging to do. I recently got this gem: "What kind of breading do you use on your wings?" I had the server answer, "standard wing breading." I just can't be bothered with shit like that.
5. When a group of people come in for a birthday and expecting us to make a custom cake for you on the spot. Nope. We are using our desserts by the slice. The amount of time required to make a cake is in the hours. Make, bake, cool, cut, decorate, and you want it now? Seriously?!
6. Adding salt and pepper at the table before you taste it, and then bitch it is too salty. That's on you.
7. Modifying a special is a pain in the ass, and I don't allow it. For example, I premade Quasidias, and they were premixed with peppers and onions. A server was informed that they were premade at the start of her shift and would make no modifications. She came back with no onions and proceeded to give an attitude. I slammed the bowl on the service counter and said, Fish them out bitch." It is special, and I will not modify a premade item. Chicken Cacciatore has onions in the sauce. Do not ask for no onions.
8. Guests delay an order by carrying on conversations, being on their phones, and ignoring the server. We use the table to generate revenue. If you want to carry on and not order food, sit in the bar area.

9. Guests who try to order things that are not on the menu. This one is just not going to happen. Asking for a different vegetable of the day instead of what we have is a good example. I will not cut up another vegetable or cook off another kind of pasta during a service just for you.
10. Rude people in general. Do you want free food? Go to the food bank. We are not a charity. If you're going to be nasty and insulting, stay home. Nobody wants s to put up with your shit.
11. Last-minute changes to reservations. This one always gets me. I had a lady book for 25 persons and showed up with 45. She was an absolute bitch about it and expected us to accommodate an extra 20 people with no advance notice during a Saturday dinner rush. Are you fucking kidding me?! Naturally, she was rude and belligerent to the staff the whole time and made a scene. Stay the fuck at home if you are going to be like that. Order pizza.
12. Eat all your food and then complain about it, like Karen and her husband with the steak incident or the loser complaining about not being a hand-packed burger. You want it for free. If it were that bad, you would not have eaten it.
13. Complain you got sick from our food. Bullshit. The chances are you got it from home. It blows my mind the unsafe handling practices at home. Not cleaning your cutting board between uses, leaving meat out too long, defrosting your meat with hot water, and the list goes on and on. We are professionally trained and follow proper handling, so the likelihood of improper handling is smaller.
14. You want us to cook outside food for you because you want to be difficult and not like what is on the menu and made-up allergies. No way. We track our inventory because, in the unlikelihood of a bad product, we know it came from if there is ever a health unit investigation. Your outside food ruins the system as it is not in our supply chain. We do not know where you got it, and we are not taking it. If you want that item, make

it a home. No reputable restaurant will entertain that garbage. It is also a health violation.

A friend of mine works at the meat counter at the grocery store. A customer came back and screamed in his face because he got sick from the meat he purchased at the store. After a ten-minute temper tantrum and screaming session, the truth came out.

The meat was purchased four days prior and was left on the counter for two days before cooking and eating. The customer assumed the store left it out at room temperature all the time, and it was safe to do so. Nope.

He explained the procedures involved in food handling and storage in a fifteen-minute conversation. Meat and other refrigerated items must go back in the refrigerator within 2 hours of purchasing it or using it. When you buy groceries, take them right home, and put them away. You can go out to eat afterwards or socialize with your friends.

After this explanation and the realization, it was their fault, they still wanted a refund. Dream on.

There is a list of things servers do to annoy us in the kitchen as well. You can find this list on many online sites and several variations. I added as to why we hate that. These behaviours are just as inconsiderate and stupid in most cases, and you will see why.

1. Bad attitude. We are not here for your abuse. Truthfully, I can replace a server a lot faster than a line cook. When push comes to shove, your ass will be out the door first.
2. No knowledge of the menu. Oh my god, learn it. It avoids headaches and stupid questions.
3. No communication. I like to know how many open menus there are. It means how many customers have menus in their hands. Allergies are important. Please give us the essential facts and details only.
4. Servers jamming the kitchen. Jamming the kitchen fucks the whole operation. Jamming happens when a server goes to several

tables, takes the orders, and puts them in simultaneously. Proper service procedure is to put the orders in one at a time and have breaks in between. Tables of 10 or more require two chits or order entries. The chits only hang so far down.

5. Complaining about tips is another one that just irritates me. Tips are earned. Take care of your guests, don't be rude, don't let the drinks run dry or the empty plates stack up. Be attentive.
6. Letting orders sit in the window is just as bad as jamming the kitchen. You are leaving food in the pass, and it prevents us from getting the other tables out. I went outside of a particular restaurant and found a server smoking. I informed the server his table's food was up. I got this excuse which almost caused me to be homicidal. "I can't run my food because I am too busy taking care of my tables." Running your food is taking care of your tables. Sitting on your ass and having a cigarette during the dinner rush is not! Run your fucking food!
7. Taking food that is not yours is a sure-fire way to piss me off. The chit you entered is put in the pass with the food for a reason. The chit has the table information and the food that goes with it. Treat it as a checklist. When I have food in the window with the chit, it is for that table. I don't give a flying fuck if you ordered the same item. It is not yours. Yours will be up when it is ready. Keep your goddamned hands off the food until it is verified it is yours. No exceptions. Taking it is fucking up my service and another customer's table.
8. They are demanding an order after you put it in. Tables are cooked according to what comes through on a first-come, first-serve basis. The exception is when I can kill the bill quickly. For example, if I have a steak medium well and two fish and chips orders, I can get the fish and chips out quicker, and we will execute and expedite that order while the steak cooks. Fish is a lot faster than a steak.
9. Servers calling out orders in my kitchen. The chef calls them out and nobody else. We have a system, and I will enforce it. I am in charge, not you.

10. Talking to my brigade rather than me. I am the chef; you speak to me. It is my kitchen, and I am in charge, not the fry cook.
11. Complain it is hot in the kitchen. Honestly, what was your first clue? Deep fryers are at 375 F, and charbroilers are at 550 F and up. Do you say It's hot? You are so observant.
12. Ordering personal food during a rush. Give your head a shake. The customers come first. You can wait for your break.
13. Excessive modifications. A burger with no onions, no lettuce, no tomatoes, no sauce, and no pickles. Did you mean plain? Seriously, I don't need to read a novel. Know your menu and use your head. Use the quickest route. It took you extra time to write it, and it takes us extra time to read it.
14. Entering the wrong information and missing items on the chit and expect us to fix it in seconds after the items have been delivered to guests. You missed a burger, and I am supposed to have it cooked in 10 seconds. Yup, sure, no problem. I will manipulate time just for you.

It is reasonable and understandable why we get annoyed. The things that annoy us are common sense and common courtesy. Violating the boundaries is never cool. You have some of your own.

On another note, I find it annoying when I go out to eat, and the menu contains the same bullshit lie as most places. "Our homemade BBq sauce" Bullshit. It came out of a jug, and you bought it. Just because you added brown sugar to it doesn't make it homemade. Case closed.

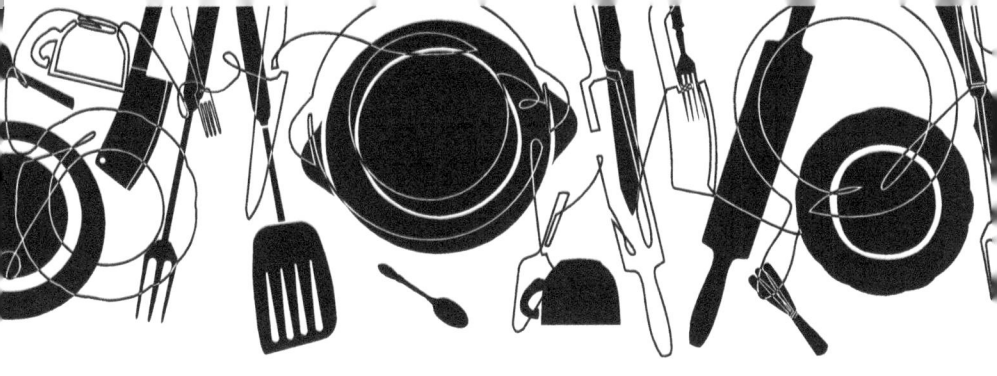

Chapter 26

We are going to change gears now. I want to get the message out that cooking is a life skill. Everyone should learn it, so I have some essential recipes and ways to encourage learning at home. We like to eat, and it should be fun and enjoyable as well as a family activity. You must know how to make meals for yourself and enjoy the food.

Cooking is not women's work or for gay men. Let's get that out of the way right now. If you are alive, you eat. You eat; cooking is for you. Case Closed.

There are so many options available to you from different ethnicities to a wide variety of fruits, vegetables, and meats. The world is full of great food. I always suggest trying it before passing judgment.

It is like anything; you didn't know you liked chocolate until you tried it. So why deny yourself another treat without trying it first. Your tastes will change as you age. There was a time I was not too fond of beets, pears, blueberries, steak and kidney pie, but I enjoy them now, to name a few.

* * *

I took an interest in the baking department first. Mom was an excellent baker. She baked for us all of the time when I was younger. I found it to be a good bonding time as well. I like that environment, and I try to have that in my kitchen, even professionally. Yes, we can be inappropriate and joke too.

I enjoyed eating the desserts she made, and I wanted to know how to make them. That is pretty much what started me off in the kitchen. Your parents will not be around forever to do those things for you. I feel it is essential to take the initiative to learn how to make your meals for the future.

You never know what the future holds, and you need to fend for yourself. We already covered that dining out every night is not feasible for the average person and can get quite expensive. You probably don't want to eat frozen dinners and canned pasta for the rest of your life, either. It is no life for your children either. I know that most people are not gourmet cooks at home, and there are lots of fast and easy ways to make meals. The soup companies have recipes and ideas on their cans as well as the internet. The internet has lots of great recipes and videos on food preparation.

For our purposes, I will give you some of the basics. I will not cram culinary school into this section because I don't think you will finish reading. I will show quick ways to make some popular items at home, stretch your leftovers into other meals for the family and grab and go lunches for work or school.

Let's make a list of things to have at the ready at all times. Get a cutting board, a decent set of knives that keep a good edge. If you buy professional knives like Wusthof or Henkel, never put them in the dishwasher. The detergent can break down the rivets and damage the handle and the edge of the blade. Always wash by hand and never put them in the sink of soapy water as someone can get a nasty surprise like the student in my culinary class. It was deep, and he required a hospital visit. Respect your knives like any other tool.

Baking needs like flour, eggs, butter and sugar are always great to have in the house. Seasonings like salt, pepper and garlic are a must. Nobody likes bland food. Engage with the family so that it becomes a bonding moment and a teaching moment too.

When they get older, it creates memories as well. When I eat chilli, meat pies, bangers and mash and mince and tatties, it brings me back to when we used to go to my grandpa's place. He made the best Scottish food.

When I bake, I remember the things Mom taught me as well. When they are gone, memories are all we have left. Make them enjoyable, and when you make those items, it is as if they are there with you again. The good memories come back, and with the food you enjoyed growing up too. It is worth holding on to and passing on to your family. You can make it as good or pretty damn close.

* * *

I suggest braising or baking more significant amounts of the protein and then portioning the leftovers and freezing them. When I buy a family pack of chicken breasts, I will season them and bake them on a parchment paper-lined baking sheet. Why use parchment paper? Less mess. The parchment paper gets the oils and baked on mess instead of your pan. Remove the baked items and throw away the parchment paper. Your pan will require a quick wipe rather than scrubbing it.

The recipes I am giving you are standard and generic, and you can adjust the seasonings to your tastes or use other recipes. The idea is to show how easy it is and get you started if you don't cook at home. It's great for teaching kids too. Always encourage safe storage and food handling when cooking. Wash your hands with soap and water between tasks as well as utensils and cutting boards.

OVEN-BAKED CHICKEN BREASTS.

8 Chicken Breasts
Vegetable or Canola Oil
2 tbsp Salt
1 tsp Pepper
1 tsp Garlic
1 tsp Paprika

Note: You can always use a premix like cajun seasoning instead of those listed. It's your kitchen, your rules.

1. Place chicken in a bowl and add enough vegetable oil to coat chicken
2. Add seasonings and ensure an even coat on the chicken.
3. Place them on the parchment paper-lined sheet smooth side up.
4. Bake at 400 F for 17-20 minutes.
5. Use a meat thermometer. Chicken parts are done at 165 F. Always insert the probe in the thickest part.
6. Remove from oven and place on a cooling rack.
7. Serve with your favourite sides.
8. Always put away leftovers within 2 hours of being cooked in the fridge or freezer in appropriate containers.
9. Label and date containers.

You made leftovers. They are perfect for making quick and easy meals for later. Cut them in strips or freeze them individually. The best idea is to use small bags and have one breast per bag for a fast and easy thaw. Always date your bags and use oldest first. Also, use plastic containers if you will use them for a family meal, freezing one portion per person in that container. For example, four persons freeze four breasts together. Use masking tape and a marker to date those items.

Some quick meal ideas include Chicken stir fry or fajitas, chicken breast on your salad with cheese and bacon, chicken cacciatore, chicken caesar wraps, or a chicken club. Endless possibilities. Get creative.

There is no excuse for eating out of a vending machine or the cafeteria now, is there? All you have to do is make the vegetable or get the wraps. Quick and easy.

BRAISED BEEF

Beef Roast (You can use pork or lamb as well)
Salt
Pepper
Garlic
Paprika
Rosemary
Thyme
2 Carrots
2 stalks Celery
2 Onions
Red Wine (optional)
Water or beef stock

1. Preheat oven to 350 F
2. Wash carrots and celery in the sink under cold water. Cut and peel onions, peel carrots. It is always an excellent habit to rinse your produce. It grows in fields and will have dirt on it.
3. Cut the carrots, celery and onions (mirepoix) into chunks and place them in the bottom of a roast pan.
4. Place roast in the pan on top of vegetables (mirepoix) fat side up.
5. Season the roast with salt, pepper, garlic, paprika, thyme and rosemary. (Premixed seasonings for beef are okay too.)
6. Fill the pan with water, red wine or beef stock about an inch and a half to 2 inches deep.
7. Place a digital meat thermometer with a cord in the beef and leave the digital unit on the counter.

8. Set the thermometer to the desired doneness and place beef in the oven. If you don't have a preset thermometer, no worries. You can always remove the lid and check periodically.
9. Braise for 2 hours and check the doneness with a meat thermometer.
10. Remove from heat when the desired doneness is achieved. This method will ensure a juicy roast from the liquid and steam circulating in your roasting pan if you like it well-done.
11. Let it rest for at least 10 minutes.
12. Strain the liquid in a pot and make gravy by adding roux to the hot liquid. Whisk until smooth. (Roux is equal parts butter and flour. Melt butter in a pan and add an equal amount of flour to the butter. Example 4 oz of butter and 4 oz of flour)
13. Slice beef ¼ inch thick for service against the grain, as previously discussed in this book.
14. Portion leftover and freeze for future use in strips ½ inch wide about 6 oz per serving: label and date.

There are many ideas for leftovers, including beef stew, Philly beef, stir fry, fajitas, stroganoff, pot pie, wraps, beef salad, shepherd's pie, beef pasta, etc. Get Creative.

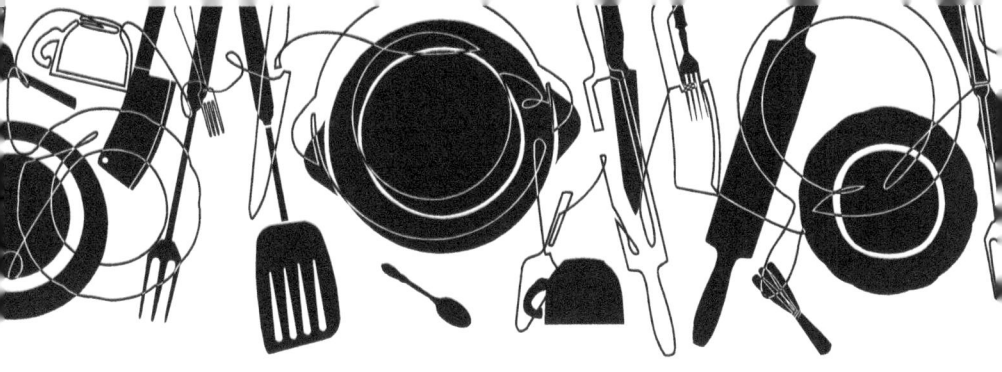

Chapter 27

Let's move onto childhood favourites. I am talking about grilled cheese but let's step it up a bit. Old favourites include Macaroni and cheese, chicken tenders, spaghetti and meatballs, alfredo, chilli (we already covered it, but it is important), meatloaf, mashed potatoes, lasagna, french fries.

I will keep them simple so that the kids can join in on the action. Keep it entertaining and engaging and a little fun. If kids get bored, they lose interest. We want them to learn this stuff. Give praise to a job well done. It builds confidence, and they will like to learn more. There are countless things they can try to make.

I will quickly touch on kids' parties. Kids want to play and have fun. If you are going to serve hotdogs, cut them in half. The result of every party I have attended with younger children is the same—half-eaten hotdogs all over the place. Lead by example as well; eat half at a time. You have little eyes that want to be like you and want a whole one because you have one in your hand. They will eat half, leave it somewhere and play. Always keep the portions small on everything, even cake and ice cream. There will be less waste and mess to clean up later. Another good practice is strategically placed waste bins.

I also suggest simple cookies and cakes for dessert: chocolate chip cookies, Oatmeal Raisin, Peanut Butter Cookies and simple chocolate or vanilla cake to begin. We want them to be good at it and enjoy it. Food is fun. We are not making future chefs unless they want to go that route, but terrific future parents and self-sufficient adults. They will have the skills to feed themselves and their future families.

A significant passing grade is a person who can make a great meal on a date night and entertain friends in style. The party host that rocks it in the kitchen will lead to rocking it elsewhere. That goes for everyone. Single people who are reading this: pay attention. Someone who cooks, cleans, and entertains in style goes to the front of the line. We will cover wine pairings in a bit. It shows style and class. That gets you to the top of the list.

Ask yourself this: What is more impressive- the person who pays for a meal at the restaurant or the one who can make restaurant-quality at home with wine pairings, apps and all the fixings? The latter, right? Dining out is a treat, but I am yours if I can have it at home all of the time. The more you know, and the more adventurous you are, the more marks you get. You're a keeper. You serve gourmet every day.

GRILLED CHEESE SANDWICH

Butter
Bread
Cheese

Sounds about right. Let's step it up. I like to use different cheeses in mine. Get creative—Mexican cheese with pico or salsa and sauteed peppers and onions. Perhaps an Italian version with Mozerella, parmesan, Asiago and salami, Prosciutto, Mortadella, Capicola, or any other Italian deli meat.

A German version- grainy mustard, bratwurst, sauerkraut, Muenster cheese on a pretzel bun. Make a Canadian version made with Canadian Bacon, cheddar cheese and tomato on a thick-cut homemade loaf.

BECHAMEL SAUCE

4 cups Milk
7 oz Butter
7 oz Flour
Salt
Pepper

1. Melt butter on low to medium heat in a pan and add flour, stirring until a smooth paste and tiny bubbles form. Remove from heat.
2. Heat milk until tiny bubbles form. Add roux and gently stir it in until it forms a sauce. Note: the sauce should always coat the back of the spoon when dipped in liquid.
3. Add salt and pepper to taste.

MACARONI AND CHEESE

Use Macaroni, fusilli or shells. Make a note of the failure with Cavatappi or Scoobi Doos from earlier. Let's not repeat that mistake, and let's not use 3-month-old sauce either. Ewww. It's gourmet, my ass.

Pasta (An excellent way to see how much you need is to pour uncooked pasta in the pan you will use to the halfway mark. Pasta will expand when cooked, and you will be adding the sauce to fill it.)

Cheese (Lots and several different kinds)
Bechamel Sauce
Bread Crumbs

1. Preheat oven to 350 F
2. Make a cheese sauce with Bechamel and season to taste. Add your favourite cheeses. Mozerella will give it strings, cheddar is traditional, and Swiss adds flavour. I like Monterey Jack, Pepper Jack, 3 State Cheese Blend, Mexican Cheese; it all works. It's your kitchen and your rules. Do not add too much cheese to the sauce. It should be a little thicker and have a smooth consistency. Use about 2 ½ to 3 cups of cheese with the bechamel sauce from above.
3. Set aside
4. Boil Pasta to el Dente approx 8 minutes.
5. Drain and put on a tray to cool and lightly oil. DO NOT RINSE.
6. Put pasta in a large mixing bowl, add cheese sauce and gently fold it in so that the sauce coats all of the pasta. Add a little sauce to the bottom of the pan and empty the bowl into the pan.
7. Cover with bread crumbs and a little shredded cheese.
8. Cover with tented aluminum foil and bake for 45 minutes to an hour.
9. Remove from oven and serve.

The kids will love to help with this one. It is a favourite. Adding the cheese to the sauce and gently stirring can be fun. Kids love to mix things. Always supervise what they are doing in the kitchen but let them have a little fun too. Always ensure safety rules of no running and hand washing and be mindful of hot pots and pans as well as sharp knives.

CHICKEN TENDERS OR NUGGETS.

Boneless chicken breasts or thighs
Buttermilk
Salt
Pepper
Garlic Powder
All-Purpose Flour
Bread Crumbs

1. Preheat Oven to 400 F
2. Cut chicken into strips against the grain and set aside—cover chicken.
3. Set up a station for breading. Flour, buttermilk and bread crumbs in separate bowls.
4. Dredge chicken in flour and shake off excess.
5. Dip Chicken in buttermilk
6. Coat chicken in breadcrumbs and place on parchment-lined baking sheet.
7. Bake for approx. 13-15 minutes.
8. Remove from heat and dip in your favourite sauce, and enjoy. These tenders beat the drive-thru. It will save money too. Make it enjoyable for the kids to make and enjoy. Add oven-made fries as well.

FRENCH FRIES

Russet (Idaho Bakers) or Multi-purpose potatoes like Yukon Gold.
Sea Salt
Canola Oil or Vegetable Oil

1. Wash potatoes in the sink and remove excess dirt if present. I prefer to leave the skins on as it adds character and flavour to the fries.
2. Cut potatoes with a fry cutter or by hand in strips. The thicker they are cut, the longer it will take to cook. 3/8 to ½ inches is ideal.
3. Soak fries in cold water for an hour. It will remove some of the starch and prevent browning.
4. Set deep fryer to 325 F
5. Strain fries and pat dry with paper towels.
6. Place fries in a deep fryer for 4 minutes.
7. Remove and place on a parchment-lined tray.
8. Turn up the deep fryer to 375 F
9. Cook for 4 minutes
10. Let fries drip.
11. Season with sea salt or your favourite fry seasoning and serve with your favourite sandwich.

MEATLOAF

2 pounds ground beef
Bread crumbs
2 eggs
Salt
Pepper
Garlic
Two small onions, small dice
Ketchup or BBQ Sauce (My advice is BBQ Sauce)

1. Preheat oven to 425 F
2. Combine beef, bread crumbs, eggs, salt, pepper, garlic, onions in a bowl
3. Mould beef into a loaf pan
4. Bake for 1 45 minutes
5. Glaze with barbecue sauce and bake another 15 minutes
6. Check internal temperature and ensure it is 160-165 F
7. Slice and serve with your favourite sides.

MASHED POTATOES

Red skin, Yukon Golds, or white potatoes. (I love red skin or Yukons myself, and I always leave the skins on.)

Butter
Milk
Salt
Pepper
Garlic

1. Wash potatoes in the sink and remove dirt from skins.
2. Cut into one-inch size chunks and place into a pot with cold salted water.
3. Bring the pot to a boil and reduce to medium heat.
4. Continue to cook until potatoes are fork-tender. This means the fork slides right into the potato easily, but it still has some structural integrity (Not mush)
5. Drain in a colander.
6. Place potatoes into a mixing bowl or stand mixer
7. Add butter and milk slowly as you mix to maintain consistency without being too soft.
8. Add seasonings and slowly beat them in.
9. Remove from bowl and serve.

Chapter 28

One of my favourite cuisines is Italian. It is easy to make and is always a crowd-pleaser. Italian food is comfort food. I love the sauces, the cheese, the pasta, garlic bread with cheese and a terrific wine for the occasion to share with family, friends, a date or anyone. Having pasta makes everything right, even after a shitty day. Kids love it, and it is fun to eat. For the love of god, please teach them to wind the spaghetti on their fork with a soup spoon. There is less mess, and it shows class.

Take your fork, pick up some spaghetti, place the fork's tines into the bowl of the soup spoon, and wind the pasta clockwise on the fork. Stop when all of the spaghetti strands are wrapped around the fork. With not rinsing the pasta, the sauce will stick to the pasta, ensuring full flavoured bites.

SPAGHETTI AND MEAT BALLS

MEATBALLS

½ to 1/3 cup Bread crumbs
½ cup Milk
1 onion small diced
2 pounds ground beef
(Half ground pork works excellent and is a preferred Italian mix)
2 eggs
2 tsp Salt
1 tsp Pepper
1 tsp Garlic

1. Preheat oven to 425 F
2. Combine ingredients in a bowl
3. Form into 1 ½ inch balls and place 1 inch apart on a parchment-lined tray.
4. Bake for 15 to 20 minutes
5. Check with a meat thermometer for 160-165 F
6. Add to pasta bowls with pasta and tomato sauce. 4-6 per person
7. Enjoy!

TOMATO SAUCE

2 – 28 oz cans of whole tomatoes
2 tsp Salt
1 tsp Pepper
2 tsp Garlic
2 tbsp Olive Oil
1 medium-size onion
1 tsp Basil
½ cup White wine (Chardonnay, Pinot Grigio or Reisling)

1. Crush tomatoes in a bowl
2. Sweat onion over low heat in a stockpot with salt, pepper, garlic and olive oil until onions become translucent
3. Add tomatoes, basil and cook over medium to low heat for about an hour, stirring occasionally.
4. Add White wine
5. Cook another half out over low heat, stirring occasionally.
6. It is always good practice to keep this in the freezer or fridge. Tomato sauce is a Mother Sauce. It has a purpose for many things and is always a great sauce to use as your go-to sauce.

SPAGHETTI

Salty water
Spaghetti

1. Boil salted water
2. Add pasta
3. Cook until al dente about 8 minutes
4. Do not throw pasta at the wall or the fridge. Taste it.
5. Strain pasta. DO NOT RINSE
6. Add sauce
7. Mix and garnish with 4-6 meatballs
8. Add cheese and enjoy with garlic bread with cheese and a glass of wine.

ALFREDO SAUCE

¼ Butter
1 cup Heavy Cream
1 tsp Garlic
1 cup Parmesan
½ tsp Nutmeg
Salt to taste
Pepper to taste

1. Melt butter in a pan
2. Add garlic and saute until aromatic
3. Add heavy cream and stir into garlic
4. Add parmesan and nutmeg and gently stir until thickened
5. Add Pasta and coat with sauce
6. Pour into a platter and enjoy.

MEAT LASAGNA

Oven ready lasagna noodles
1 pound ground beef
Tomato sauce
Mozerella cheese
Asiago cheese (optional)
Parmesan Cheese

1. Preheat oven to 350 F
2. Brown ground beef in a pan, drain and set aside.
3. Spoon tomato sauce in the bottom of the lasagna pan to coat bottom
4. Cover sauce with a layer of lasagna noodles
5. Sprinkle cooked ground beef to cover noodles

6. Layer with sauce
7. Add cheeses
8. Cover with lasagna noodles
9. Repeat the process until top of the lasagna pan.
10. Do not go over the top of the pan.
11. Generously cover with sauce
12. Generously cover with cheese
13. Bake in the oven for approximately 1 hour.
14. Serve with salad and garlic bread as well as wine.
15. Enjoy

On a side note, I find Italian makes a great date night at home. Italian is the number one choice for date night worldwide. Going out for Italian with family and friends is fun, but with a special someone, it is magic.

Avoid pizza on date night. Pasta Bolognaise (meat sauce), Alfredo, Tomato Sauce, garlic bread, salad, and wine make the night special. This section will help you entertain restaurant-quality Italian nights at home. Pay attention to the wine section in the next chapter. A quick search online will enhance it.

Chapter 29

We covered some essential foods with the previous chapters, and I gave you enough to encourage creativity and explore new dishes. I didn't want to write a cookbook, but I wanted to encourage everyone to get in the kitchen and cook together. I love sharing a kitchen. Food is to be shared from start to finish.

Now for the best part of dinner and entertainment. Wine. I have my wine certification and will abbreviate it for you to enjoy with family, friends or dates.

There are lots of great wine-growing regions around the globe. Canada, United States, Italy, France, Australia, Chile, Spain, Argentina, New Zealand, Germany, Portugal, South Africa, China, Romania, Hungary, and Russia.

The most famous types of wines are listed below. There are more, but we will stick to these varieties as they are familiar and for simplification. Wine and cheese are the best companions, and you can try several with different cheese and crackers.

All wines have sulphites as it is a natural byproduct in the fermentation process. When you see a wine with no sulphites, it means no added sulphites. Sulphites are innate in some foods, and they are also used as a preservative to maintain colour and shelf life and prevent bacterial growth.

Sulphites are in canned and frozen fruits, juices, jellies and preserves, jams, syrups, dried fruits, dehydrated vegetables and starches, tomato pastes, condiments, vinegar and alcoholic beverages and maybe in other foods as well.

Tannins are from the stems, skins, seeds and wood barrels used in the ageing process of wines. It creates a dry sensation in the mouth. I am giving a cliff note version of the wines and pairings. IF you have a local winery near you, I will encourage you to go on a tour and sample what they have. There are lots of flavour profiles for each wine and winemaker. It is worth an afternoon with friends. I would recommend the same for a brewery or distillery as well.

When choosing wine, please do not ask the clerk for something fruity in wine. All wine is fruity. It takes on other fruit flavours as it is fermented. My best suggestion is to say what you are doing with it. It is easier to pair it with food. You will see the general fruity undertones and pairings in the typical wines I chose in the coming pages.

First, let's set up how to taste and drink wine properly. It is not something you guzzle and chug like frat boys at a kegger. Wine is about sipping and savouring. When you sip, you get the flavour profiles. When you pair it with food, you bring out more flavour and compliment the food.

Red wine glasses will have larger bowls to contact the oxygen and bring out the tannins in the wine. This is called aerating, and it will reduce the bitter taste. Red wine goes to the back of your mouth for the full effect of the flavour.

White wines have a U-shaped bowl and keep the wine cooler longer. White wine should be served chilled for maximum flavour. There are sparkling wine flutes for keeping the bubbling and preserve the taste.

To drink wine, let it breathe. Fill the glass about halfway and swirl the wine. Swirling exposes the wine to oxygen and brings out the flavours. Never fill to the brim. Fill it halfway. It allows aerating and flavour. You can always have more.

The older the wine, the better the taste is not always true. The ageing occurs in the fermentation process. It would help if you drank or consume the wine within two years. Red wines can go up to 5 years.

When you open the wine, smell it. If it smells terrible, like a wet dog or a strong vinegar smell, the chances are it will taste bad. Cork rot, improperly corked; if you pour it and it is brown, it is over oxidized. If it is "off-tasting," you will spit it out. It's nasty. It will be like trying to eat spoiled meat. It cannot be done without spitting it out. Can you go down on your partner without a shower? Nasty smelling cock or pussy is not getting serviced. That is a hard pass. Take a fucking shower. Treat wine like that too.

Ask for a recommendation at the restaurant or wine store. Pair your wine with its purpose and food. A short generic description and pairing are coming in the following few pages. There are lots of pages online with this information and suggestions. When you aerate the wine by swirling, enjoy the aromas. Taste in small sips and roll it over your tongue and swish it around your mouth and give your taste buds a complete workout. A good wine will leave a lasting flavour in your mouth.

Red wines should be chilled about 10 minutes before service to get the full flavour. White wines should be chilled and served 41 F to 48 F.

RED WINES

CABERNET SAUVIGNON

Cabernet Sauvignon is one of the most well-known red wines. It is a full-bodied and flavoured wine high in tannins and acidity. In hotter regions like Australia, it will have a jam-like taste. Whereas in cooler climates, it has tones of blackberry or black cherry notes. A good comparison would be a fully ripened strawberry with a full flavour.

When pairing this wine with food, it is excellent with game meats, beef, lamb and other fatty meats. It also goes well with rich, creamy sauces. I love this wine, and it is my go-to red wine.

CABERNET FRANC

Cabernet Franc is orifginated from Bordeaux, France. It is lighter, so I would say a bright red strawberry but not fully ripened. It has a medium body flavour. Depending on the climate, it can take on flavour profiles, including raspberries, chocolate, bell peppers, and violet aromas.

This wine pairs well with grilled meats like steaks, chops, lamb, pork, beef, mushrooms, chicken, and fish and, of course, cheese and crackers.

BACO NOIR

Baco Noir is a medium body wine but tastes almost like a full body wine with undertones of blueberry, blackberry, and plum flavours.

This wine pairs well with burgers, pizza, lasagna, pasta, meatloaf, soul food such as ribs, baked beans, BBQ foods like beef brisket and full flavoured condiments like Dijon mustard and horseradish. I love this one myself for its flavour and multipurpose pairings.

SYRAH

Syrah is also known as a Shiraz and has a high content of tannins. Its flavour profile can contain blackberry, chocolate, licorice, mocha, and black pepper, depending on the region in which it is grown. This wine is often most blended with Cabernet Sauvignon.

Food pairings include game meats, grilled meats, stew, barbecued chicken, burgers, lamb, and cheese.

SANGIOVESE

Sangiovese is red Italian wine. It has a medium body. It is my go-to for pasta night. Chianti is a Sangiovese from the Chianti region of Italy. Chianti is my favourite Italian wine, hands down.

Sangiovese pairs well with rare meats, chicken, mushroom, tomato sauce, so I refer to it as my pizza and pasta wine. Italian night it is this wine, accept no substitutions.

MALBEC

Malbec is a full-body red wine with a dark berry finish and undertones with a smoky finish. Notes can contain cocoa, black pepper, blackberry, plum, raspberry and blueberry. It has a medium tannin to it as well.

Food pairings include lean red meats, blue cheese and rustic flavours like mushrooms and other earthy vegetables. It pairs with dark poultry, buffalo, duck, pork and lamb.

PINOT NOIR

Pinot Noir is light in tannin and light-bodied red wine with strawberry, raspberry, cherry undertones, and usually higher than other light-bodied wines. It is generally grown in cooler climates.

This wine pairs well with salmon and other fatty fish. It's great with roasted chicken, pasta, duck, and stews. All wine is excellent with cheese. Try them all.

MERLOT

Merlot is a trendy light red wine used to blend with other wines such as a Cabernet Merlot. Merlot has a medium tannin and has a wide variety of flavours depending on the growing region. It can take on flavours: strawberry, plum, blackberry, black cherry, and chocolate.

Food pairings include beef that has been grilled or roasted, blue cheese, Cheddar, chicken grilled or roasted, mushrooms, lamb. Pork, pork loin and roast pork.

WHITE WINE

CHARDONNAY

Chardonnay is a green grape used to make white wine. Chardonnay is neutral and picks up its flavours during fermentation. Depending on the region, it can range from buttery to apple, pear, citrus, peach, hazelnut: Mango and other tropical undertones.

Food pairings include cheese, of course, shellfish like lobster, clams, and shrimp. Upon further digging, I found it is excellent with popcorn, nuts, mac n cheese, grilled cheese and caramel corn: your kitchen, your rules.

RIESLING

Riesling is a full-body white wine that can be dry or semi-sweet. Late harvest Rieslings are sweeter. Depending on the growing region, it can take on green apple, peach, pear with honey notes.

Food pairings include light fish, Asian food, chicken, tuna, salmon, crab, cheese such as Swiss. It is excellent with Alfredo sauce, Do not use tomato sauce with this one. That is more for red wine. On a personal note, I prefer this as one of my summer white wines: this and a Gwertraminer. There are blends of these two wines, and it's a taste bud party in your mouth.

PINOT GRIGIO

Pinot Grigio is a trendy white wine refreshing with melon, mango, green apple, pear, and a hint of honey. It is a light-bodied white wine and pairs well with light and fresh items.

Pairings include summer items like salad, chicken, seafood, lighter pasta, sushi, crab, and other warmer climate offerings. Think summer.

GWERTRAMINER

Gwertraminer is my other favourite white wine. When fermented, it can take on exotic flavours like lychee fruit and apricot. It has a higher sugar content and is off-dry. This wine is an excellent summer drink, as previously stated with the Riesling.

Gewurztraminer pairs well with spicy Asian dishes, Muenster cheese, duck, egg dishes, shellfish and is highly recommended with Thanksgiving dinner. It serves well with Thai, Indian, Szechuan and spicy foods.

SAUVIGNON BLANC

Sauvignon Blanc is crisp, dry and refreshing and can take on flavours like green bell peppers, grass, grapefruit, pears, and asparagus. New Zealand is known for its Sauvignon Blanc. It has high acidity and low sugar content.

Sauvignon Blanc pairs well with goat cheese, asparagus, artichoke, zucchini, light fish like sole, mild vinaigrettes, summer salads, oysters and pesto.

ZINFINDEL

Zinfindel has a robust flavour and makes an excellent full-body red wine. It is also a great Rose or a White Zinfindel and is very popular as it has a higher sugar content which can be more alcoholic during the fermentation process. It can take on flavours of blackberry and pepper, depending on the growing region.

This wine pairs well with meats like beef, lamb, pork and other grilled meats. A White Zinfindel pairs well with fresh and roasted vegetables, fish, salads, and cheese like Blue Cheese.

White Zinfindel should be served cold. It can even compliment a light dessert like a sorbet.

When cooking with wine, there is a straightforward rule most chefs will use, and it is:

If you wouldn't drink it, don't cook with it.

I hate using cooking wine. It is salty, and I find it is shit. I will not use it. I have been forced to use it at some places where I have worked in the past. We are not baiting deer with a salt lick. I had to make a Beef Bourignon with it, and it was salty. I was not happy with it. I typically love this dish. It is hearty and very comforting. Now I brought it up; I will give you the recipe. The wine you choose will help you in cooking or outright fuck you. Choose wisely. Stay away from cooking wine.

BEEF BOURIGNON

1 tbsp olive oil
Half pound bacon thinly sliced into one-inch strips (cut across)
2 pounds stewing beef. Cut into bite-size pieces.
(You can use the leftover meat from a roast for this too.
Reduce cooking time about 15 minutes)
Salt to taste
Pepper to taste
2 tbsp tomato paste
2 onions cut into thin strips
1 pound carrots peeled and cut into half coins ¼ to 1/3 inch thick
1 750 ml bottle of red wine such as Pinot Noir or Cabernet Sauvignon
2 cups beef broth
Garlic to taste
1 pound sliced mushrooms
3 tbsp butter
3 tbsp flour

1. Preheat oven to 300 F
2. Cook the bacon in a skillet with oil.
3. Remove the bacon and reserve the fat.
4. Sear the beef in bacon fat, salt pepper, and garlic. Set aside. (If using leftover meat, you can skip this step. Please make sure they are bite-sized pieces)
5. Cook carrots and onions, mushrooms in the fat with salt, pepper, and garlic until soft. Set Aside.
6. Melt the butter and combine with flour to make a roux.
7. Combine all ingredients in a roast pan and place in oven covered for about 1 hour.
8. Serve with toast and a bottle of the wine you used and enjoy.

In closing - Never be afraid to try food or drink. There are so many things to try out there. Please do it. You can't go wrong. Some things you may not like, but there will be plenty you will. Your family and friends will love it. Are you stumped for dinner? There are apps out there, and with a quick search with ingredients on hand, you can have a gourmet meal. Keep your favourites recorded. With all of the choices, you should not have to settle for mundane and tasteless food or cheap takeout and drive-thrus.

Nobody asked you to be a gourmet chef but if you are- own it. I wrote this book for anyone who works in the industry. It is also for whoever wants to be entertained and learn how to make great food at home. Your spouse will thank you. I did a poll online and asked the following:

Person A has a decent job, is a good cook and entertains in style at home and is fun.

Person B makes a little more money and likes to order takeout a couple of times a week and doesn't cook, but they are also fun.

Who would you prefer?

The results: 73 % of people voted for person A, whereas only 15% voted for Person B, and 12% were OK with either one.

Are you surprised? I wasn't.

Never stop learning and never stop tasting and sipping. There is too much enjoyment to have. Expand your palate and your culture. Try as many cuisines as you can, whether entertaining at home or going out to eat or if you work in the industry.

Bon Appetite!